CW01266732

A POET IN LOVE

A POET IN LOVE

Peter Davey

ARTHUR H. STOCKWELL LTD
Torrs Park Ilfracombe Devon
Established 1898
www.ahstockwell.co.uk

© Peter Davey, 2009
First published in Great Britain, 2009
All rights reserved.
No part of this publication may be reproduced
or transmitted in any form or by any means,
electronic or mechanical, including photocopy,
recording, or any information storage and
retrieval system, without permission
in writing from the copyright holder.

British Library Cataloguing-in-Publication Data.
A catalogue record for this book is available
from the British Library.

Arthur H. Stockwell Ltd bears no responsibility
for the accuracy of information recorded in this book.

This book is dedicated
to Mari.

ISBN 978-0-7223-3957-2
Printed in Great Britain by
Arthur H. Stockwell Ltd
Torrs Park   Ilfracombe
Devon

Contents

Information on the Illustrations	7
Acknowledgements	9
Chronology of the Life and Times of John Keats	11
People Who Appear in This Story	19
Wentworth Place, Hampstead, Known as Keats House	23
Bo-Peep, Hastings	27
Preface	30
Isabella Jones, the 'Hastings Lady'	51
Frances Brawne (Fanny)	79
British Artists, Poets and Writers: Contemporaries of John Keats	156
Keats Poems Mentioned in This Book	168

Information on the Illustrations

Wentworth Place (Keats House), Hampstead, London, built by Charles Armitage Brown & Charles Wentworth Dilke, in 1815. This is where Keats met Fanny Brawne in Oct/Nov 1818. And where he lodged with Brown in his part of the house. Fanny and her mother nursed Keats here in 1820, before he left England for Rome, Italy.
(From a watercolour by Mari Davey 1998) – Illustration No: 1.
Page 33

Bo-Peep, Hastings, as it was in Keats time. He came here on holiday in 1817, and met with Mrs Isabella Jones (The Hastings Lady). Note the River Asten running along the shoreline, as it did at the time.
(From an oil painting by Mari Davey 2002) – Illustration No: 2.
Page 33

The Mill House, Bedhampton, Sussex, where Keats and Brown stayed with the miller John Snook in January 1819. Whilst there Keats wrote the poem 'The Eve of St Agnes'. He spent his last night in England there in September 1820.
(From a watercolour by Mari Davey 2007) – Illustration No: 3.
Page 34

The Keats-Shelley Memorial House and Museum, Rome, Italy.

Piazza di Spagna (the Spanish Steps). Where Keats died on 23 February 1821. Keats and Joseph Severn rented rooms on the second floor.
(From a watercolour by Mari Davey 2008) – Illustration No: 4. Page 34

John Keats – from a miniature by Joseph Severn, 1819.
(National Portrait Gallery, London) – Illustration No: 5. Page 35

Frances (Fanny) Brawne – from an Ambrotype.
(Keats House Museum, Wentworth Place, Hampstead) – Illustration No: 6. Page 36

George Keats – from a miniature by Joseph Severn.
(Keats-Shelley Memorial House. Piazza di Spagna. Rome, Italy) – Illustration No: 7. Page 37

Thomas (Tom) Keats – from a miniature by Joseph Severn.
(Keats-Shelley Memorial House. Piazza di Spagna. Rome, Italy) – Illustration No: 8. Page 37

Frances (Fanny) Keats de Lanos – from a portrait by her son, Don Juan Lanos y Keats.
(Keats House Museum, Wentworth Place, Hampstead) – Illustration No: 9. Page 38

A sample of Fanny Brawne's handwriting. Page one of a letter to Keats' sister Fanny, January 1821.
(Keats House Museum, Wentworth Place, Hampstead) – Illustration No: 10. Page 39

John Keats – by Joseph Severn, 1823. (A Posthumous Portrait)
(National Portrait Gallery, London) – Illustration No: 11. Page 40

Acknowledgements

Without those who have researched, studied and written about John Keats before me, this book would never have come into being. Their work, along with my own research and my own feeling for the poet, has inspired me over the two years it has taken me to write this book.

I owe the biggest debt of gratitude to those who have trodden the path before me, and I have leant most heavily on the three following works: Robert Gittings' *Keats* (1968) and *John Keats: The Living Year* (1954), and Maurice Buxton Forman's *The Letters of John Keats* (1935). Other books used as sources of material are John Middleton Murry's *The Poems and Verses of John Keats* (1949), Fred Edgcumbe's *Letters of Fanny Brawne to Fanny Keats* (1937), and *Nelson's Encyclopaedia* (1963 edition).

I also wish to thank those who have supported me and given practical help during the period of my studies and writing: Kohji Aoyama, the Japanese author of *Keats: My Genius* (1998), who set me upon this exciting road; the President of the Suffolk Poetry Society, Michael Bannister, a published poet and writer, who gave up his time to proof-read and advise on this manuscript; Catherine Walling, Assistant Curator of the Hastings Museum of Local History for her help with my research into Bo-Peep and The New England Bank inn; my wife, Mari, for her patience and sympathetic ear, and for her artwork: the paintings of Keats House, Wentworth Place Hampstead; the shoreline at Bo-Peep, Hastings; the Mill House, Bedhampton, Sussex; and the Keats-Shelley Memorial House,

Piazza di Spagna (the Spanish Steps), Rome; the London Metropolitan Archives for permission to reproduce images from the collection in Keats House; the National Portrait Gallery, for the portraits of John Keats by Joseph Severn; the Keats-Shelley Memorial House, Rome, for the portraits of George and Thomas Keats by Joseph Severn. For help with the research into Wentworth Place, I should like to thank Mr Kenneth Page, the information officer at Keats House.

Chronology of the Life and Times of John Keats

1795	Oct. 31	John Keats' birth, Finsbury, London. Exact location unsure.
	Dec. 18	John Keats is christened at St Botolph's, Bishopsgate.
1797	Feb. 28	George Keats' birth.
1799	Nov. 18	Thomas Keats' birth.
1801	Apr. 28	Edward Keats' birth (died in infancy).
1803	Jun. 3	Frances (Fanny) Mary Keats' birth.
1803–11		John Keats is educated at John Clarke's School, Enfield.
1804	Apr. 16	Thomas Keats, John's father, is killed in a riding accident.
	Apr. 23	Thomas Keats is buried at St Stephen's, Coleman Street.
	Jun. 27	Keats' mother, Frances, marries William Rawlings at St George's, Hanover Square.
1804–10		The Keats children live with their grandmother, Alice Jennings, at Edmonton.
1805	Oct. 21	Nelson is killed at the Battle of Trafalgar.
1810	Mar.	Keats' mother, Frances, dies of tuberculosis; on 20 Mar. she is buried at St Stephen's.
1811		The madness of King George III – George IV becomes regent. Keats begins his apprenticeship with Dr Thomas Hammond.

1812		Keats writes his 'Imitation of Spenser'.
1813		Keats meets and becomes friendly with Joseph Severn.
1814	Dec.	Keats' grandmother, Alice Jennings, dies; on 19 Dec. she is buried at St Stephen's.
1815	Feb. 2	Keats writes the sonnet 'Written on the Day That Mr Leigh Hunt Left Prison'.
	Jun. 18	The Battle of Waterloo.
	Oct. 1	Keats enters Guy's Hospital as a student.
1816	May 5	Keats poem 'O Solitude' is published in *The Examiner*.
	Jul. 25	Keats sits exam to qualify as an apothecary.
	Nov.	Keats is introduced to Benjamin Robert Haydon.
	Dec. 1	Keats meets Leigh Hunt, with Charles Clarke at Hunt's cottage, Vale of Health, Hampstead.
	Dec.	Keats meets Shelley and Horace Smith at the Hunts'.
1817	Mar. 3	Keats' first book of poems is published by Olliers.
	Spring	Keats meets Taylor and Hessey (new publishers), also Woodhouse and Bailey.
	Apr. 15	At Carisbrooke, Isle of Wight, Keats begins Book 1 of *Endymion*.
	May 10	At Margate with his brother Tom, Keats reads over the lines of *Endymion* written so far.
	May 16	Keats goes alone to Canterbury.
	May 18	Keats meets Isabella Jones at Bo-Peep, West Hastings.
	Jun. 10	Keats is back in London, at Well Walk, Hampstead.
	Sep. 5	Keats is at Oxford with Benjamin Bailey.
	Oct. 4	Keats visits Stratford-upon-Avon with Bailey.

1817	Oct. 5	Keats returns from Oxford to Well Walk, Hampstead.
	Oct. 8	Unwell, Keats is confined to his house; he writes to Bailey.
	Nov. 6	Princess Charlotte dies in childbirth.
	Nov. 28	*Endymion* is finished at Burford Bridge.
	Dec. 28	Haydon's 'Immortal Dinner' is attended by Keats, Wordsworth, Lamb, Kingston, Monkhouse, Joseph Ritchie, and John Landseer.
1818	Jan. 3	Keats calls on Wordsworth at Mortimer Street.
	Jan.	*Endymion*, Book 1 is sent to Taylor and Hessey.
	Jan. 27	Keats hears Hazlitt's lecture on Shakespeare and Milton at the Surrey Institution.
	Feb. 4	Keats writes 'Sonnet to the Nile' in competition with Leigh Hunt and Shelley.
	Feb. 5	*Endymion*, Book 2 is finished and copied.
	Feb. 10	Keats attends Hazlitt's lecture.
	Feb. 17	Keats attends Hazlitt's lecture.
	Feb. 27	*Endymion*, Book 3 is finished and copied.
	Mar. 14	Keats joins Tom at Teignmouth; *Endymion*, Book 4 is finished and copied.
	Mar. 21	First *Endymion* preface and dedication are sent to Taylor and Hessey.
1818	Apr. 10	Reynolds proofs second *Endymion* preface.
	Apr. 26	*Endymion* is published.
	Apr. 27	The long poem 'Isabella' is finished.
	May 11	Keats returns to Hampstead from Teignmouth.
	Jun. 22	George and Georgiana, just married, leave London for America; Keats and Brown travel with them as far as Liverpool.

1818	Jun. 25	On a visit to the Lake District with Brown, Keats calls on Wordsworth at Dove Cottage, but he is out.
	Jun. 30	The travellers reach Carlisle.
	Jul. 1–31	The Scottish walking tour.
	Jul. 11	Keats visits Robert Burns' cottage and tomb.
	Aug. 7	Unwell, Keats returns to London by sea.
	Aug. 18	Keats arrives at Hampstead.
	Sep.–Dec.	Keats nurses the dying Tom at Well Walk.
	Oct. or Nov.	Keats' first meeting with Fanny Brawne.
	Oct.	Keats renews his acquaintance with Isabella Jones.
	Dec. 1	Tom Keats dies; John moves to Wentworth Place.
	Dec. 7	Tom Keats' funeral takes place at St Stephen's.
	Dec. 25	Keats spends Christmas Day with the Brawne family – supposed engagement to Fanny.
1819	Jan. 21	With Brown at Chichester and Bedhampton, Keats writes 'The Eve of St Agnes'.
	Feb.	Keats returns to Wentworth Place; he has a sore throat.
	Feb. 13–17	Keats writes 'The Eve of St Mark' (unfinished).
	Feb. 22	Keats stays in town with Taylor. There is a snowstorm.
	Feb. 23	Keats breaks up with Isabella Jones.
	Apr. 11	Keats meets and walks with Coleridge in Hampstead.
	Apr.	Keats writes 'La Belle Dame Sans Merci', 'Ode to Psyche' and 'Ode on a Grecian Urn'.
	May	Keats writes 'Ode to a Nightingale'.

1819	Jun.	Keats' sore throat persists; he is very unwell.
	Jul.	Keats goes to the Isle of Wight with James Rice, and they are joined by Charles Brown. They begin a joint project: 'Otho the Great'.
	Jul. 25	Keats is supposed to have composed the sonnet 'Bright Star'.
	Aug. 12	Keats goes to Winchester accompanied by Brown; 'Otho the Great' is finished.
	Aug. 16	The Peterloo Massacre takes place at St Peter's Field, Manchester.
	Sep.	At Winchester, Keats is working on 'Hyperion'.
	Sep. 10–15	Keats goes to London on a money-raising quest for his brother George.
	Sep. 15	Keats returns to Winchester. 'Ode To Autumn' is written; he revises 'The Eve of St Agnes'.
	Oct.	Keats begins writing 'The Cap and Bells'.
	Oct. 8	Keats leaves Winchester for London, to live for a short time at 25 College Street, Westminster.
	Oct. 15–16	Keats returns to Hampstead, to live with Charles Brown, Fanny Brawne and family next door. Keats becomes vegetarian.
	Dec.	Keats is unwell – flare-up of his sore throat.
1820	Jan.	'Ode on a Grecian Urn' is published in the *Annals of Fine Arts*; his magical spell of poetry-writing comes to an end.
	Feb. 3	The fatal consumption (tuberculosis) begins; blood from his lungs fills his mouth.
	May 4	Keats leaves Wentworth Place for lodgings near Leigh Hunt at 2 Wesleyan Place, Kentish Town; Brown lets out Wentworth Place.

1820	May 7	Keats accompanies Brown on the smack to Gravesend as he leaves to begin his holiday in Scotland. This was the last time that they saw each other.
	May 10	'La Belle Dame Sans Merci' is published in *The Indicator*. Death of George III, who was declared to be mad in 1811. Hugely disliked by the people, the Prince Regent became George IV.
	Jun. 22	Keats' illness worsens; Leigh Hunt takes him into his own home and summons a doctor.
	Jun.	In the last week of June, Keats second book is published: *Lamia and Other Poems*.
	Jul. 1	The *Literary Gazette* prints 'Ode to a Nightingale', 'The Mermaid Tavern' and the ode 'To Autumn'.
	Jul. 20	'To Autumn' appears in the *Literary Chronicle*.
	Jul. 29	The *Literary Chronicle* prints 'Ode on a Grecian Urn'.
	Aug. 12	Keats returns to Wentworth Place and is nursed by Fanny Brawne and her mother.
	Aug.	*The Indicator* prints four stanzas of 'The Cap and Bells'. Reviews of Keats' new poems are printed in the *New Times*, *The Examiner*, the *Edinburgh Review* and *The Quarterly*.
	Sep. 13	Keats leaves Wentworth Place, Hampstead, to begin his journey with Severn to Italy.
	Sep. 17	Keats boards the *Maria Crowther* in the London Docks and moves downriver to Gravesend.
	Sep. 18	The *Maria Crowther* sails from Gravesend and encounters a storm in the Channel.
	Sep. 20	Becalmed off Dungeness, Keats goes ashore.

1820	Sep. 28	The *Maria Crowther* puts in at Portsmouth for repairs; Keats and Severn visit the Snooks at Bedhampton. This was Keats' last night in England.
	Sep. 29	The voyage is renewed, but there are contrary winds. Keats and Severn go ashore at Studland Bay or Lulworth Cove (Gittings suggests Holworth).
	Oct. 21	The *Maria Crowther* arrives at Naples, where the ship is put into quarantine.
	Nov. 1	Keats and Severn disembark at Naples.
	Nov. 8	Keats sets out by carriage for Rome.
	Nov. 15	Keats arrives at Rome.
	Dec. 10	Keats suffers a relapse, from which he does not recover.
1821	Feb. 23	Keats dies at the Piazza di Spagna apartment on the Spanish Steps.
	Feb. 26	Keats' funeral takes place. He is buried in the Protestant cemetery outside the Aurelian Wall, near the Pyramid Tomb of Caius Cestius.
	Feb.	Napoleon Bonaparte dies on St Helena.
1822		Percy Bysshe Shelley is drowned in Italy. Some of his remains are buried near Keats in Rome.

People Who Appear in This Story

Abbey, Richard – the Keats' siblings' guardian.
Brawne, Frances – Fanny's mother.
Brawne, Margaret – Fanny's sister.
Brawne, Samuel – Fanny's father.
Brawne, Samuel (junior) – Fanny's brother.
Brown, Carlino – Charles Brown's son.
Brown, Charles Armitage – Keats' friend and part owner of Wentworth Place.
Bentley, Mr and Mrs – the Keats' brothers' landlords at Well Walk, Hampstead.
Clarke, Charles Cowden – Keats' teacher and lifelong friend.
Cotterell, Charles – Miss Cotterell's brother.
Cotterell, Miss – a consumptive passenger aboard the *Maria Crowther*, during Keats' voyage to Italy.
Cox, Jane – the Reynolds' beautiful East Indian cousin.
Cornish, Mrs – a friend of the Abbeys.
Dilke, Charles – the son of Charles Wentworth Dilke.
Dilke, Charles Wentworth – Keats' friend. Writer and editor.
Dilke, Maria – Charles Dilke's wife.
Dilke's, Mr and Mrs – Charles Wentworth's father and mother living at Chichester.
Dilke, Sir Charles Wentworth – Member of Parliament. Dilke's grandson.
Frogley, Mary – Keats' girlfriend (an old flame).
Forman, Maurice Buxton – Keats' biographer.

Gittings, Robert – Keats' biographer.
Graham, William – the journalist who faked an interview with Joseph Severn.
Haslam, William – Keats' 'oak friend'. Solicitor.
Haydon, Benjamin Robert – Keats' friend. Historical Painter.
Hazlitt, William – Keats' friend. Writer, lecturer and artist.
Hessey, James – Keats' publisher, in partnership with Taylor.
Hunt, Leigh – Keats' friend. Poet, writer and editor.
Hunt, Thornton – Leigh Hunt's eldest son.
Jeffrey, Marian – Mrs Jeffrey's daughter. Was she in love with Keats?
Jeffrey, Mrs – the Keats boys' landlady at Teignmouth.
Jennings, John and Alice – Keats' grandparents.
Jennings, Midgley and Margaret – Keats' uncle and aunt.
Jones, Isabella – a woman romantically associated with Keats.
Keats, Frances – Keats' mother, née Jennings, later Rawlings.
Keats, Frances (Fanny) – Keats' sister.
Keats, George and Thomas – Keats' brothers.
Keats, John – the poet.
Keats, Thomas – father of John, George, Tom, and Frances.
Lindo, Louis – Fanny Brawne's husband. His name changed to Lindon at the time of their marriage.
Llanos, Valentin – Frances (Fanny) Keats' husband.
Lockhart, John – columnist for *Blackwood's Edinburgh Magazine*.
O'Callaghan, Donat – Isabella Jones's old sponsor.
O'Donaghue, Abigail – Brown's Irish servant, and mother of his son, Carlino, born out of wedlock. She married Brown later, possibly in Ireland.
Perrins, Rose – a lady who wrote in support of Fanny Brawne.
Reynolds, John, Charlotte (the mother), Jane and Marianne – friends of Keats. John was a solicitor, poet and writer.
Rice, James – Keats' friend. Lawyer (often unwell).
Severn, Joseph – Keats' friend. Portrait painter. He accompanied Keats to Italy.

Snook, John – Charles Dilke's brother-in-law. Miller. Owner of the Mill House, Bedhampton.

Taylor, John – Keats' publisher, in partnership with Hessey.

Wilson, John Gibson – columnist for *Blackwood's Edinburgh Magazine*. With Lockhart he was responsible for attacks on Keats and his poetry. He published under the pen-name of Z.

Woodhouse, Richard – Keats' friend. A lawyer, and a reader for the publishers Taylor and Hessey.

Wylie, Mrs – mother-in-law of George Keats.

The doctors attending John Keats during his illness were Dr Bree, Dr Lambe, Dr Rodd and, when in Rome, Dr James Clark.

Wentworth Place, Hampstead, Known as Keats House

Wentworth Place was built as a joint venture between Charles Armitage Brown and his friend Charles Wentworth Dilke during the years 1814–16. It was completed by February 1816, but stood empty until the October of that year, when Charles Wentworth Dilke and Charles Armitage Brown took up residence. The house was one of the first properties to be built in the Lower Heath Quarter of Hampstead. William Dilke, the younger brother of Charles Wentworth, built his house adjacent to Wentworth Place soon afterwards. Dilke's grandson, Sir Charles Wentworth Dilke, recalled, 'It was my great uncle William that painted the name at the gate of Wentworth Place.' (from Harry Buxton Forman's biography of Keats). There is said to have been yet another property nearby occupied by a member of the Dilke family. How the cost of the project was shared is unknown, but as Dilke's part of the property was the greater his portion of the finance is likely to have been larger than Brown's.

Keats House is near the bottom of Keats Grove, formerly John Street. From the front elevation it has the appearance of a detached house, but in Brown and Dilke's time an unbroken wall separated the building into two parts. Keats said that a wall separated him from Fanny Brawne, but today both parts of the house are connected by internal doors.

Steps led to a front door between two large casement windows. This door led to the larger, 'eastern', part of the house, which was occupied by Charles and Maria Dilke. Brown, a bachelor, lived in the smaller part to the west. His accommodation included front and back sitting rooms on the ground floor, with bedrooms, front and back, above them. There was a small spare room or box room, where a guest might stay overnight. Keats began to visit the house in 1817, after he had been introduced to Charles Wentworth Dilke by John Hamilton Reynolds, the poet solicitor, who was attached to the Leigh Hunt circle of friends.

In December 1818, after the death of Keats' brother Tom, Brown invited Keats to 'keep house' with him. Keats paid Brown £5 per month (which is roughly equivalent to £200 today), and they had an agreement that Keats would contribute half the cost of the liquor bill – usually wine. Overall Keats lived in the house for fourteen months, over a period of almost two years (December 1818 to September 1820), firstly with Charles Brown and later (in 1820) with Fanny Brawne and her mother.

When Keats lodged there with Brown, he had the use of the front sitting room, which he called the front parlour. The window of this room gave a view of the front garden and John Street. From his bedroom at the rear of the house Keats had a view of the smaller garden to the north.

Both parts of the property include basement rooms, which were used as kitchens and pantries and a small servants' quarters. Maybe, during her time in Brown's employment, Abigail O'Donaghue occupied a basement room in that part of the house. In a letter to his brother George, Keats mentions hearing Abigail in Brown's bedroom, which was just across the landing from his.

Brown transferred his part of the house to Dilke's father on 18 June 1822 and left England for Italy that same year. Charles Wentworth Dilke, his wife Maria and son Charles left the property on 3 April 1819 and moved to Westminster for Charlie's education. Dilke let his part of the house to Mrs Brawne, then a widow, and her three children – Fanny, Margaret and Samuel. The Brawnes had briefly rented Brown's part of the house whilst Keats and

Brown were on their walking tour in the North and Scotland in 1818.

Fanny Brawne's mother died on the steps of Wentworth Place in December 1829 after an accident with a candle. By March 1830, Fanny with her sister and brother had left the house.

After Keats' death, his sister Fanny and Fanny Brawne became friends. Fanny Keats had married Valentin Llanos, a Spanish diplomat and writer. Fanny, now Mrs Llanos, lived in Brown's part of the house from 1828 until 1831.

The house was almost continually occupied from then until it opened to the public as the Keats Memorial House on 9 May 1925. There were several occupants of note during the nineteenth century:

The painter and illustrator Henry Courtney Selous lived here from 1835 to 1838.

Later, Miss Chester, a retired actress who in her younger days had been a favourite of George IV, converted the house into one dwelling and added the large room seen to the left when facing the house from the road. She used this room as a dining room when entertaining; now the 'Chester Room', as it is known, is used to house artefacts of Keats and Fanny Brawne – letters, manuscripts, etc.

A piano manufacturer, Charles Cadby, lived in the house from 1858 to 1865.

He was followed by a physiologist, Dr William Sharpey, who was in residence from 1867 to 1875.

Then came the Reverend Dr George Currey, Master of Charterhouse, in 1876.

The house was named Wentworth Place in 1818 by Dilke's brother William and Mrs Maria Dilke, while her husband was absent, taking a rest cure for some illness. Brown's part of the property was for a short time in 1838 known as Wentworth Cottage, but by 1842 the property again became Wentworth Place. It then went through several name changes: Lawn Cottage, 1843–4;

Laurel Cottage, 1845–9, and then again Lawn Cottage, 1849–67. From 1868 it was known as Lawn Bank until it was officially renamed Wentworth Place in 1924. This is the name that Keats and his friends would have been familiar with, although now it is often referred to simply as Keats House.

The Heath Branch Public Library is next door to the house, and it occupies an area that would once have been the kitchen garden of Wentworth Place. The library was opened to the public on 16 July 1931, and the artefacts now in Keats House were originally on display in the front part of this building.

The house is decorated and furnished in the style of the 1820s.

Bo-Peep, Hastings

Bo-Peep is the name now given to an area of St Leonards. On a 1746 map there appears a substantial property called Bo-Peep House; in the same area in the early eighteenth century there was a well-used inn known as The New England Bank. It was here that Keats came on holiday for a few days in 1817. The name of the inn was later changed to Bo-Peep, and the building was demolished in 1844 to make way for the West Marina railway station.

It's likely that Bo-Peep was recommended to Keats by his friend Benjamin Haydon, the famous painter, who had taken a holiday there in 1814. Lord Byron came to Hastings on holiday with his sister Augusta in the same year. Haydon, in his journal, mentioned that the Martello towers opposite the inn housed wounded soldiers brought back to England from Spain. He also wrote, 'on returning to London, riding on the outside of the coach I had one of the 95th, a desperate rifleman by my side'.

At the time, The New England Bank was a notorious haunt for smugglers. It was one of a very few buildings between Hastings and Bulverhythe, and it was said to be a popular stop for travellers going to Bexhill. A Hastings guidebook of 1794 describes The New England Bank as a public house by the roadside, where company may have an excellent dish of tea, good cream 'alfresco and enjoy a fine prospect of the sea and Beachy-Head from the Hill beside the house'. It was from this same area that the two Misses Matthews sent Keats a present of a large shell, a gift which he immortalised in his poem 'On Receiving a Curious Shell'.

It was during this short holiday to Bo-Peep that Keats first met the mysterious 'Hastings Lady', Isabella Jones. At the time, the River Asten did not flow out to sea at its present mouth, west of the bathing pool, but ran parallel to the shoreline to a sluice somewhere near the west end of Caves Road. (The river can be seen as it was then in Mari's oil painting, reproduced on page 33.) The area around Hastings at the time that Keats was there was thinly populated by probably not more than 3,000 people.

Elizabeth Barrett Browning wrote these lines on the death of John Keats (taken from *Aurora Leigh*):

> . . . the man who never stepped
> In gradual progress like another man,
> But, turning grandly on his central self,
> Ensphered himself in twenty perfect years
> And died, not young, – (the life of a long life,
> Distilled to a mere drop, falling like a tear
> Upon the world's cold cheek to make it burn
> For ever;) . . .

Preface

> From his earliest days.
> His life was blighted by
> Harsh realities, and death
> Dogged his waking hours.
> And yet, the nervous spirit
> Within him rose above mere
> Earthly bonds, to leave us
> The wonders from his brilliant pen.

Nine months after meeting Fanny Brawne, Keats wrote this description of her: 'Small and delicate, lively, but unsentimental. With a good figure and movement, and fashionably dressed hair . . .'. He also wrote the following lines.

> Deep blue eyes, semi-shaded in white lids,
> Finished with lashes fine for more soft shade
> Completed by her twin-arch'd ebon brows;
> White temples of exact elegance,
> Of even mould, felicitous and smooth;
> Cheek fashion'd tenderly on either side,
> So perfect, so divine, that our poor eyes
> Are dazzl'd with the sweet proportioning,
> And wonder that 'tis so, – the magic chance!
> Her nostrils small, fragrant, faery-delicate;
> Her lips, I swear no human bones e'er wore
> So taking a disguise.

John Keats and Fanny Brawne met in the October or early November of 1818, whilst he was still involved with the mysterious Isabella Jones.

John had known other women before he met Fanny, although he never admitted to being in love with any of them.

Isabella was a mystery woman then and remains so to this day. It's possible that she was one of the many Whig (Liberal) hostesses of the time. Isabella, an educated, sophisticated woman, moved in different circles to Keats. She was attached in some undefined way to a rich seventy-year-old Irishman, Donat O'Callaghan, who is likely to have been her sponsor.

Although Keats mentions the 'Hastings Lady' in correspondence to his brother George in America, he never once named her. (One hundred and thirty-five years after the poet's death, Robert Gittings, the Keats biographer, identified her from letters that passed between James Hessey and his partner in a publishing business, John Taylor.) Keats admitted that she was an enigma to him!

Their affair began with their first meeting at Bo-Peep, where John had gone on his own for a short break. Their clandestine meetings took place over three days in Whit week, May 1817. The meetings were conducted under the nose of Isabella's jealous old sponsor. (Very few biographers have written about what took place at that time; some even deny the existence of Isabella. It was left to Gittings to bring her to life in *John Keats: The Living Year* (1954) and his Keats biography, *Keats* (1968). No one knows for sure what happened between Keats and Isabella during those three days. Keats did not disclose it, but he was a man who loved to walk and explore new places, so it's unlikely that he spent the time within the confines of The New England Bank inn. Reading between the lines of the poems 'Hush, Hush! Tread Softly!' and 'You Say You Love', both inspired by that exciting interlude, I conjecture that Isabella alternately encouraged and rebuffed the passionate poet.

Keats met her again in October 1818, and from then on they often spent time together in her upstairs apartment in Queen

Square, London. At the end of that October, in a letter to George, he mentions a physical attraction towards her, and that they had kissed. Writing about the second meeting, he said he 'felt it would be living backwards not to kiss her again'. It seems she felt differently about it and tactfully put him off, which puzzled him.

All through Keats' life, girls flit in and out.

In 1815 he had an interest in a dark-haired, beautiful girl, Mary Frogley, whom biographers have termed 'an old flame'. Mary was a member of a poetry group which was headed by her cousin, George Felton Mathews.

When at Teignmouth, Devon, with his brother Tom, who was there for his health, they lodged at the boarding house of a Mrs Jeffrey, who had three daughters. Marian, the eldest, seems to have been attracted to Keats. After he had returned to London, she wrote a poem complaining of unrequited love.

Keats' fellow poet and friend, John Hamilton Reynolds, had two sisters, Jane and Marianne, both of whom had a flirting connection with John and his brother George.

John was also much taken with their cousin, Jane Cox, an East Indian beauty. He wrote to George that thoughts of her kept him awake at night. 'I should like her to ruin me,' he added.

Of the women he knew, only one can be said to have inspired any poetry of importance, and that one is Isabella Jones. For that alone she should, I believe, not be excluded from the Keats story. Although he fell in love with Fanny Brawne, nothing good poetry-wise came from their relationship, except for a few lines full of bitterness.

Fanny and her mother enjoyed a full social life. They went to the local military balls and danced in the Long Room at Well Walk, where Fanny met and danced with Frenchmen escaping Napoleonic persecution – Frenchmen of excellent manners and etiquette, well able to charm a young girl. The Long Room dance hall in Hampstead was also frequented by military officers from the nearby barracks.

Keats viewed Fanny's popularity through jealous eyes. His

*Illustration No: 1. Wentworth Place (Keats House), Hampstead, London.
(From a watercolour by Mari Davey, 1998)*

Illustration No: 2: Bo-Peep, Hastings. (From an oil painting by Mari Davey, 2002)

Illustration No: 3. The Mill House, Bedhampton, Sussex.
(From a watercolour by Mari Davey, 2007)

Illustration No: 4. The Keats-Shelly Memorial House and Museum, Rome.
(From a watercolour by Mari Davey, 2008)

Illustration No: 5. John Keats – from a miniature by Joseph Severn, 1819.
(National Portrait Gallery)

*Illustration No: 6. Frances (Fanny) Brawne – from an Ambrotype.
(Keats House Museum)*

*Illustration No: 7. George Keats – from a miniature by Joseph Severn.
(Keats-Shelly Memorial House)*

*Illustration No: 8. Thomas (Tom) Keats – from a miniature by Joseph Severn.
(Keats-Shelley Memorial House)*

Illustration No: 9. Frances (Fanny) Keats de Lanos, from a portrait by her son, Don Juan Lanos y Keats. (Keats House Museum)

[JAN. 15. 1821.] N°. 5.

My dear Miss Keats

I am almost ashamed to write to you though I have been waiting for above three weeks to do so, but I hope you will forgive me, for it is not quite my fault. On the 23rd of December, Mr Brown received a letter from your brother in which he desired that someone would write to you, to say

Illustration No: 10. A sample of Fanny Brawne's handwriting: page one of a letter to Keats' sister Fanny, January 1821. (Keats House Museum)

Illustration No: 11. John Keats, by Joseph Severn, from a posthumous portrait, 1823. (National Portrait Gallery)

friend Charles Dilke commented, "He don't like anyone to look at or speak to her." Keats' men friends, seeing the damaging effect she was having upon him, accused her somewhat cruelly of being nothing more than 'a vulgar suburban flirt'. As Benjamin Haydon, a painter of huge historic pictures, wrote in his journal, "He did not bear the little sweet arts of love with patience." Keats, resentful at the way his mind was being affected by the association, took himself off to the Isle of Wight. He felt unable to work on his poetry whilst he was near her. From there he wrote strange, accusing letters; in reply she tormented him, telling of late-night parties and dancing. He wrote:

> Ask yourself my love whether you are not very cruel to so have entrammelled me, so destroying my freedom, will you not confess this in a letter you must write immediately?

There seems little doubt that the early stages of disease were beginning to affect his mental state. His sore throat returned time after time, and the mercury he had taken to reduce the symptoms of some other mysterious complaint had brought on a highly nervous condition – 'I am in a complete cue-in fever; My mind is stuffed like a cricket ball' – and yet at this time he was entering the most prolific period of his poetic life. Robert Gittings wrote of this period as 'The Living Year' – a year at the end of which his working life was done, for in February 1820 he entered the twelve months of disease that would finally bring about his untimely death.

> I am free from Men of Pleasures cares
> By dint of feelings far more deep than theirs.

Most of Keats' problems with the establishment and critics of the day stemmed from his association with Leigh Hunt. This, however, should be balanced against the benefits of their friendship.

The way that Keats was regarded in the public eye hardly changed after his death. The public was indifferent, and he was in danger of being forgotten. Then, in 1848, the two volumes of *Life, Letters and Literary Remains of John Keats*, edited by Richard Monckton Milnes (later to become Lord Houghton) came before the public. By the publication of this, the first serious biography of the poet, readers became aware of the poetic genius that they had almost discarded. His poetry was at last admired for its romantic beauty and intellectual content; poetry-lovers were introduced to the genius of Keats. As more and more of his letters came to light – letters that were comparable in content with the poems – biographers began to reveal the true character of the poet, a character attractive to people of all ages. The letters disclose the pain he suffered at the loss of those he loved, his difficulties over money matters, his struggle to come to terms with the love of a woman, his 'wrong' feelings towards women in general, and his efforts to become accepted into the world of literature.

I believe Keats' birthday was 31 October 1795; some biographers believe it could have been the 29th. Leigh Hunt said that he was a seven-months child, and that he was born in June 1795; where this came from no one knows, and there is no evidence to back it.

Keats was seven years younger than Byron, three younger than Shelley; if he had lived a longer life, it's likely he would have met Dickens and Tennyson, for they were both born within his lifetime. It is to the writings of Dickens that we should look to understand the times that Keats lived in. The Terror of the French Revolution ended in 1795, and Napoleon appeared on the scene, but life at the level on which Keats and his friends lived continued unaffected.

Up until the age of eight, the life of John Keats was comfortable, placid and secure, but then in April 1804 his father died in a fall from his horse. His mother seems to have gone off the rails, and she remarried almost at once.

This marriage soon failed and Frances Keats left the family home at the Swan and Hoop Livery Stable and Inn. Seeing her grandchildren abandoned, Alice Jennings took them to live with her at Edmonton, then a small village to the north of London. The

Keats children's grandfather had died very soon after their father, leaving his wife, Alice, very well situated. She understood children, and her home was just what was needed to settle their lives. John Jennings, their prosperous grandfather, had left them legacies and money enough to assure them a good life and pay for their education.

Alice Jennings died in December 1814, and their appointed guardian, Richard Abbey, became central to their lives. Abbey was a staid city merchant and his ways did not extend to literature and poetry. To say that Abbey and Keats did not understand each other would be to simplify the situation.

At his school in Enfield, John Keats studied the usual subjects: history, geography, arithmetic, grammar and some French and Latin. As a youngster he was not recognised as an able pupil, and it was not until the death of his mother in February 1810 that he suddenly applied himself to his lessons. His passion for sport evaporated as he became interested in all types of books – especially those on the Greek gods and heroes.

On leaving school he became apprenticed to a local doctor-surgeon named Hammond. How and why this choice of profession came about we cannot be sure, but Richard Abbey may have used his influence and authority. Hammond's practice was situated very near to Keats' grandmother's house in Edmonton. There is no evidence of pressure, from any source, on John at the time, and he made no objection to joining the medical profession.

Employment at Hammond's practice does not seems to have been onerous, for Keats had time off to visit Charles Cowden Clarke at his old school, where he continued with his studies.

Clarke lent him books, including Edmund Spenser's *The Faerie Queen*. Keats' request for this book amused the Clarkes, for they had no notion that Keats was beginning to turn poetical. John questioned the younger Clarke, who explained the metre and form of a poem's construction.

In October 1815 John Keats became a medical student at Guy's

Hospital, and in the summer of 1816 he qualified as an apothecary. His fellow students soon realised that poetry was dominant in his studies, and his brothers already boasted that John was destined to become a great poet. Richard Abbey, ignorant of his young protégé's plans, proposed he take up a surgeon's practice at Tottenham or take over from the retiring Hammond. "I do not intend to be a surgeon, I mean to rely upon my abilities as a poet," Keats replied. This difficult conversation remained in the memories of both parties, and Abbey never forgave Keats for it.

John made his first attempt at a poem in 1813, entitling it 'Imitation of Spenser'. Most of his early works were, in part, imitations of poets that he had studied.

Charles Cowden Clarke, an admirer of Leigh Hunt, introduced Keats to Hunt's weekly newspaper, *The Examiner*, whilst he was still in school.

John saw Hunt as a champion of liberal ideas, both in politics and poetry. Hunt advocated a new way for English poetry – a break away from what the establishment considered correct. Both Clarke and Keats were caught up in Hunt's ideas.

In Hunt's 'The Feast of the Poets' appeared:

> Oh for a seat in some poetic nook,
> Just hid with trees and sparkling with a brook!

Hunt continued experimenting until, in 1816, he published *The Story of Rimini*, written whilst in Horsemonger Lane Gaol. There are those who lay the blame at Hunt's door for some of the bad in Keats' early work, but this theorising is of little importance in the overall picture of Keats' poetic life. In his poem 'Written on the Day That Mr Leigh Hunt Left Prison', Keats writes so strongly against the establishment that it appeared to some that he was about to get himself into the same trouble as Hunt; certainly the established Tory press marked him for future punishment.

After Charles Clarke had introduced Keats to Hunt in October 1816, Hunt began to find space in *The Examiner* for the young poet's work, and from that time on he gained a new circle of friends. At Hunt's cottage in the Vale of Health at Hampstead, Keats met Benjamin Haydon, Shelley, J. H. Reynolds, Vincent Novello (the organist) and others. He was able to converse there with the mighty critic William Hazlitt.

Hunt's readers began to enjoy poems such as 'On First Looking into Chapman's Homer'. In the poem 'Sleep and Poetry' Keats reveals his feelings now that the pathway to fame had opened up to him.

During the winter of 1816, living with George and Tom in lodgings in Cheapside, John revised some of his older poems and wrote new ones. Leigh Hunt together with John's brothers urged him to publish a volume; Shelley warned against it. There were many small books of poetry in circulation at the time, and Keats' book failed to attract many purchasers – proving Shelley right! Hunt, still a staunch supporter, praised the little volume in *The Examiner*. Had Keats not met with Leigh Hunt, he would have found another opening into the literary world, but surely it would have taken longer to achieve. However, the blessings of exposure in *The Examiner* were mixed: although thousands looked for it every Sunday, there were thousands more that hated it. Politics and poetry were linked in the opinion of the conservative press, and any misjudgements in private life were exposed in print, as Keats was soon to realise.

There were other problems within the Hunt circle: Leigh placed Shelley above Keats as a poet, and John was uncomfortable in the company of Shelley. Although Shelley's advice was sound, John felt uncomfortable with Shelley's morals and superior education. Keats turned to Haydon for support, Reynolds joined him, and Hunt's little group seemed on the verge of breaking up.

The publishers of Keats' first book – the Ollier brothers – turned against him. The volume had failed spectacularly and they were out of pocket. They would accept nothing more from his pen! Reynolds found him a new publisher: Taylor and Hessey of 93 Fleet Street were looking to increase the publishing side of their business, and they saw in Keats a young poet of promise. They advanced him money against the new long poem *Endymion*, in which he turned to his favourite subject, Greek mythology, for subject matter.

> A thing of beauty is a joy for ever:
> Its loveliness increases; it will never
> Pass into nothingness . . .

During the year 1817 Keats spent time away from London to concentrate on *Endymion*. He went to the Isle of Wight, Margate, Oxford and Burford Bridge in Surrey. He visited Oxford in the summer with a new friend, Benjamin Bailey, who was in Magdalen Hall studying for the Church. Whilst the budding clergyman read his books, Keats kept to his set task of writing fifty lines a day. In the sunny afternoons they rested from their labours and took boating expeditions on the Cherwell and Isis, where they read Shakespeare and Wordsworth. Wordsworth was Bailey's favourite poet, and through his friend's enthusiasm John came to admire the elder poet.

The gathering of new friends continued when he met with Charles Brown and Charles Wentworth Dilke, who had built a house together in Hampstead. It was situated a short distance from Well Walk, where Keats now lodged with his brothers at the home of Bentley, the local postman. The house was known as Wentworth Place, and it was soon to have a special place within the Keats story.

Other friends around Keats included Joseph Severn (the portrait painter), James Rice (a solicitor who liked to write verses) and Richard Woodhouse (also in the legal profession – an adviser and reader for Keats' new publishers, Taylor and Hessey).

Woodhouse appointed himself unofficial editor of Keats' poems. He collected all the works from the poet's pen that came his way, and in the future his collections were to be of great benefit to editors and biographers.

In the December of 1817, Wordsworth came to London, and

Keats through Haydon was able to meet him. At Haydon's urging, he read to him part of *Endymion*, the 'Hymn to Pan'. Wordsworth already knew of Keats, and, not a man to reveal his feelings one way or the other, responded with: "A pretty piece of paganism!"

Keats wrote that he was 'disgusted with literary men'. However, Wordsworth thought more of the young poet than Keats imagined, for he said that he believed Keats was "too good for the sorry company that he keeps".

The original bond with Hunt remained strong enough for Keats to go with him to musical supper evenings at the home of the organist Vincent Novello, in Oxford Street.

In March 1818, John was in Teignmouth, Devonshire, with his brother Tom, who was suffering from tuberculosis. Tom's doctor had advised a change of climate in a last effort to improve his health, but Tom Keats died in December 1818 after John had nursed him devotedly for several months. George Keats was not there: he had married that year and emigrated to America. In his heart John felt that George had abandoned them. It was rumoured that George had drawn on John's inheritance, leaving him in debt, but this was never proved.

Keats was now alone in London, left to make a home for himself; luckily Charles Brown came to his aid and offered him a lodging at Wentworth Place.

Soon after George's departure and Tom's death, Keats suffered further when *Blackwood's Edinburgh Magazine* began to attack his person and poetry, but the strongest blow came from the *Quarterly Review* for it was in every London reading room and was regarded as an authority. It's difficult to judge the effect on Keats from that September article. No man, however strong, could avoid being troubled by the virulent articles that were published. To soften the blow, there were several friendly reviews of *Endymion*.

During the summer of 1818, Keats had travelled to the north in the company of Charles Brown. They went on a 'walking tour' through Cumbria and on into Scotland. Whilst in the Lake District they called on Wordsworth at Dove Cottage, but they were disappointed to find him out. They visited Burns Country – his cottage and his grave. At the cottage they were pestered by an old man who said he was a guide. The man's brogue was so strong that it was difficult to understand what he said. He offered them drams of whisky, which they declined. During the walk they managed to get to Ireland, but found the place so poverty-stricken that they hastily returned to Scotland. On the road they came across the 'Duchess of Dunghill'. John managed the ascent to the summit of Ben Nevis, even though his sore throat again plagued him.

After Ben Nevis, his health began to deteriorate. At last he became too unwell to continue, and he was forced to return to London aboard a coastal smack. On his return to Hampstead he found Tom entering the last stages of tuberculosis.

After the loss of Tom, the move to Wentworth Place was exactly what was needed. He could, although grieving, at last read and write in peace and comfort.

Then a further agitation presented itself in the shape of Miss Fanny Brawne, with whom he fell in love. He had long been in love with love itself, but this was real!

He was also involved with the exotic Mrs Isabella Jones, but she was an enigma to him and beyond his reach. Miss Brawne was different; he felt himself to be on firmer ground with her.

In the June of 1819 he left London for the Isle of Wight, and from there he went to stay at Winchester for the rest of the summer. In spite of being settled in Wentworth Place and enjoying Brown's continuing kindness, he had an itch to travel abroad. He spoke of the near continent, and dreamt of Africa, but Winchester was as far as he got. He stayed there from August to October. His problem was that Mrs Brawne was now renting Dilke's half of Wentworth Place; Fanny would be just a wall away.

In the period spanning autumn 1818 to autumn 1819 he produced a set of poems and odes that were to place him on a level with the greatest writers of the age. The odes alone would have ensured his future fame – fame that he had doubted, but never entirely dismissed from his mind. These great odes are so well known that it seems unnecessary to list them here: 'Ode to Psyche', 'Ode on Melancholy', 'Ode to a Nightingale', 'Ode on a Grecian Urn' and 'Ode on Indolence'. During this time he also wrote the poems 'La Belle Dame Sans Merci' and 'To Autumn' and the sonnets 'On Fame', 'To Sleep' and others.

In February 1820 a rush of blood to his mouth revealed the dreadful truth: Keats had contracted tuberculosis. By the end of spring he appeared to be recovering, and Brown left him to go away on his usual Scottish holiday. As Wentworth Place was to be rented out for the summer, Keats was forced into a lodging at Kentish Town, which Leigh Hunt had found for him near to his own home. When he became too unwell to be left on his own, Hunt took him into his home and nursed him. The Hunts' house was noisy and overcrowded, and Leigh was himself ill, but he would not turn away a friend in need.

On 12 August a dispute arose over a misplaced letter from Fanny Brawne. Keats was overly upset, and he left the Hunts' to walk up to Hampstead. There, Mrs Brawne found him and took him into Wentworth Place.

In the July another book of poems had been published. Sales were slow, but better than his first book or *Endymion*. John was too unwell to care either way. His doctors advised going to Italy as the only chance of survival. This had to be funded, but Keats knew it would be useless to approach Abbey for a loan. The gulf between them was too great. Taylor and Hessey got up a subscription, to which those of Keats' friends as could made contributions. Enough money was raised to cover the voyage and expenses for a few months, but who would be prepared to accompany him? Brown was away and out of reach. Finally, Joseph Severn was asked, and he agreed to go.

On 18 September 1820, the brig *Maria Crowther* cast off her mooring and put to sea from Gravesend. The voyage proved rough and arduous, but the poet survived to reach Rome, where he was to be cared for by Dr James Clark, who had found the rooms for the travellers at 26 Piazza di Spagna, The Spanish Steps.

During the long journey, Keats had done his best. He appeared to be recovering, but it was heroic play-acting for the benefit of Joseph Severn and their fellow-travellers. Dr Clark used the trusted conventional treatments for tuberculosis – treatments that were doomed to fail.

Keats died on the night of 23 February 1821, and he was interred in the Protestant Cemetery at Rome on the 24th.

Isabella Jones, the 'Hastings Lady'

On Monday 14 April 1817, Keats took the Defiance, a coach bound for Southampton. His destination was the Isle of Wight. Taking Benjamin Haydon's advice, he had decided to leave London's distractions and separate himself from his brothers and friends in order to concentrate on *Endymion*. He said that the work would be a test:

> a trial of my Powers of Imagination, and chiefly of my invention, which is a rare thing indeed – by which I must make 4,000 lines of bare circumstance and fill them with poetry.

The coach rattled into Southampton, past the Bargate with its two stone lions, arriving in time for breakfast. Although excited, John was tired out from the rigours of the seventeen-hour journey. He felt anxious, nervous and lonely. Thinking to calm himself, he unpacked his bag, took out his Shakespeare folio and began reading.

Finding that it would be 3 p.m. before the ferry left for the Isle of Wight, he took up pen and paper to write a descriptive letter to his brothers, George and Tom, on the events of the journey so far.

In the afternoon of the 15th he crossed over and landed in Cowes. After disembarking he went by coach to Newport in search of a cheap lodging for the night.

Shanklin had been recommended as a good place to stay, and the next morning he travelled there, only to find that the cost of accommodation was more than he could afford. Making his way back toward Newport, he found a lodging to his liking in Castle

Road, a mile outside the town in the direction of Carisbrooke. The small boarding house was called Canterbury House. Mrs Cook, the owner, was a lady of friendly disposition, interested in her lodgers' welfare. She noticed John's attraction to a print of William Shakespeare hanging in the hallway, and she offered to put it in his room – a bright airy room with a view of Carisbrooke Castle.

On Thursday the 18th he settled down to work on *Endymion*. He had set himself a goal of fifty lines a day, and he kept to it, writing all though the morning and then taking a break to walk along the cliffs. After ten days he became exhausted by the task he had set himself. In a letter to Haydon, he wrote, as he said himself, 'like a Madman' and to his brother George he wrote, 'I'm not altogether capable in my upper storey's.' Taking a day off from *Endymion* he wrote a sonnet, 'On the Sea', then copied it out in a letter to his old friend John Reynolds.

On the Sea

It keeps eternal whisperings around
    Desolate shores, and with its mighty swell
    Gluts twice ten thousand Caverns, till the spell
Of Hecate leaves them their old shadowy sound.
Often 'tis in such gentle temper found,
    That scarcely will the very smallest shell
    Be mov'd for days from where it sometime fell,
When last the winds of Heaven were unbound.
Oh ye! who have your eye-balls vex'd and tir'd,
    Feast them upon the wideness of the Sea;
      Oh ye! whose Ears are dinn'd with uproar rude,
Or fed too much with cloying melody –
Sit ye near some old Cavern's Mouth, and brood
Until ye start as if the sea Nymphs quir'd –

At the time his plan was to complete Book 1 in the span of a month, and by concentrated writing he neared his target of 1,000 lines and sent *Endymion* off on his adventures.

Feeling tired and a little lost, his mind turned toward the mainland, and a break in Margate was soon arranged. Whilst there he planned to spend some time with his brother Tom.

Short of money, he appealed to his new publishers, Taylor and Hessey, for an advance; they seem to have been sympathetic, for on 16 May he sent a letter thanking them for £20.

On 17 May he took the ferry across to the mainland, then travelled 150 miles by coach along the treeless coastline to Margate.

At Margate Tom was already waiting at a lodging where they had previously enjoyed a holiday.

During the stay, Keats read over the first part of *Endymion* to a receptive Tom.

Soon tiring of the bleak East Sussex coast, John decided on a change of scenery. He moved on to Canterbury. He wrote to Taylor, 'the Remembrance of Chaucer will set me forward like a Billiard-Ball'.

The time spent in Canterbury can only have been a few days, for we find Tom leaving to rejoin George at Hampstead whilst Keats went off alone to spend Whit week in Hastings. He planned to stay at a resort called Bo-Peep at The New England Bank, an inn which stood on the present-day site of the West Marina railway station.

The place was almost certainly recommended by his friend Benjamin Haydon, the famous painter, who had also spent a holiday in the district. Haydon, after he had been awarded the sum of 100 guineas by the Royal Society for his great picture *The Judgement of Solomon* in 1814, had decided to take a break at Bo-Peep, and he also stayed at The New England Bank.

Haydon wrote:

> Having received my cash I set off for Hastings and took lodgings at Bo-Peep, opposite the Martello Towers, where I spent the time bathing in the sea and shooting the Gulls for sport! I was surprised to find one of the Martello Towers filled with wounded soldiers from Spain.

The inn was known to have connections with smuggling at the time, but a Hastings guidebook of 1794 describes The New England Bank as:

> a public house by the road side where company may have an excellent dish of tea, and good cream 'Alfresco' and enjoy a fine prospect of the sea and Beachy Head from the hill beside the house.

On the morning of his second day there, John set off on a long walk of discovery, finding the Valley of Ecclesbourne and continuing on to Fairlight Glen along the cliff path. He rested to partake of a light lunch, brought with him from the tavern. He stopped at a rock known as the Lovers Seat – a well-known trysting place. A story goes that the daughter of a wealthy landowner would meet her lover secretly at this spot. One day the hapless lad fell from the cliff to be devoured by the waves under the very eyes of his sweetheart. She, determined to share his fate, plunged head foremost from the rock into the sea below.

The Hastings Guide of the period describes Ecclesbourne and Fairlight:

> This is one of the most favourite spots in the neighbourhood for visitors from London, being delightfully rural, and where buoyant spirits are able to indulge in fun and frolic they would hesitate to exhibit on the thronged parade.

As he was about to continue his walk, Keats met a young woman, about his own age – or so he believed. It's likely that she was older. Although Keats had no idea at the time, she most likely knew of him. They fell into easy conversation and walked on together. She told him that she was staying at The New England Bank, where she was waiting for a friend to arrive. As they neared the tavern she implored him to take a different path as not to arrive in company.

Keats had been immediately attracted to her, and, finding himself dry-mouthed and excited, he asked her if they could walk together again the next day.

To his request she readily agreed. Keats had met for the first time Mrs Isabella Jones.

In the life of Keats, Isabella Jones is considered a dark horse; in fact, early biographers either didn't know of, or denied, her very existence. So who was Mrs Isabella Jones, and what was her social status?

It seems she was what is known as a kept woman. Certainly, the friend that she had told Keats would be arriving at the inn was a rich Irishman of some seventy-plus years of age. He was a member of a titled Whig family, by the name of O'Callaghan. Her particular friend or sponsor was Donal, or Donat, O'Callaghan, Donal being the Irish version of the name Daniel. It is also known that he had a brother with a military background – Colonel James O'Callaghan – who was a year older than Donal. James O'Callaghan had been a member of parliament in 1806 and 1807, and he was to be again in the years 1818–20. So how was Isabella connected to this family? It is possible that Mr Jones (if there ever had been a Mr Jones) was an officer in the Duke of Wellington's army, serving under Colonel James O'Callaghan. If her husband had been killed in action, it's again possible that Colonel O'Callaghan had taken the beautiful young widow under his wing; she could then have been sponsored by Donal, the unmarried brother.

Whatever the truth of it, Donal watched over her jealously. He was in the habit of spending the summer months at Hastings, and this explains the presence there of Isabella.

At other times she lived at a good address in London. She was known to give parties 'where one could meet pretty women, and . . . sensible men could show their good sense by looking at the pretty women' (Isabella's own words). She was certainly beautiful, had a lively, not to say biting, wit, and wrote an excellent hand. Her literary tastes were those fashionable in her day: she read novels of the Gothic-horror type – the counterpart of modern-day thrillers. She was interested in the poetry of Barry Cornwall, and, even at the time of her first meeting with Keats, was a particular friend of his new publisher, John Taylor. Keats was, however, completely unaware of this connection or he might have shied off!

On the third day, and after Keats and Mrs Jones had spent almost the whole of the previous day together, the carriage of Donal O'Callaghan arrived at the inn. Isabella told John that they must not be seen together by the old man. Keats was smitten; he had 'warmed with her' and kissed her. This could mean many things, from the mildest of flirtations to a possible sexual experience for Keats. What it seems to mean, in the language of the day, is that he was stirred sexually by her, but that he – or, more probably, she – thought it best to stop at kissing. This is borne out by a little poem he wrote for her to keep as a memory of their Whit-week encounter. The poem 'You Say You Love' is said to have been written in 1815, but, as it was for Isabella Jones, it can't have been. It is most likely to have been composed in the autumn of 1818. The reasoning unfolds.

You Say You Love

1.

You say you love; but with a voice
Chaster than a nun's, who singeth
The soft Vespers to herself While the chime-bell ringeth –
O love me truly!

2.

You say you love; but with a smile
Cold as sunrise in September,
As you were Saint Cupid's nun,
And kept his weeks of Ember. (Ember Days (Lent)
O love me truly!

3.

You say you love – but then your lips
Coral tinted teach no blisses.
More than coral in the sea –
They never pout for kisses –
O love me truly!

4.

You say you love; but then your hand
No soft squeeze for squeeze returneth,
It is like a statue's dead –
While mine to passion burneth –
O love me truly!

5.

O breathe a word or two of fire!
Smile, as if those words should burn me,
Squeeze as lovers should – O kiss
And in thy heart inurn me!
O love me truly!

During the day, Isabella was obliged to be with O'Callaghan, but on at least one occasion she left his bed in the night to go to John in his room. Maybe for one time only, they went together out into the gardens to walk the paths amongst the flowers and kiss by the light of the moon. The secrecy of this meeting is illustrated by the poem he wrote in October of the same year. 'Hush, Hush! Tread Softly!' was written, it's believed, in 1818 for Isabella Jones as a memento of their midnight tryst, hiding from her jealous old sponsor, Donal O'Callaghan, during the brief affair at Bo-Peep.

Song/Poem Hush, Hush! Tread Softly

1.

Hush, hush! tread softly! hush, hush my dear!
All the house is asleep, but we know very well
That the jealous, the jealous old bald-pate may hear,
Tho' you've padded his night-cap – O sweet Isabel!
Tho' your feet are more light than a Fairy's feet,
Who dances on bubbles where brooklets meet, –
Hush, hush! soft tiptoe! hush, hush my dear!
For less than a nothing the jealous can hear.

2.

No leaf doth tremble, no ripple is there
On the river, – all's still, and the night's sleepy eye
Closes up, and forgets all its Lethean care,
Charm'd to death by the drone of the humming May-fly;
And the Moon, whether prudish or complaisant,
Has fled to her bower, well knowing I want
No light in the dusk, no torch in the gloom.
But my Isabel's eyes, and her lips pulp'd with bloom.

3.

Lift the latch! ah gently! ah tenderly – sweet!
We are dead if that latchet gives one little chink!
Well done – now those lips, and a flowery seat –
The old man may sleep, and the planets may wink;
The shut rose shall dream of our loves, and awake
Full blown, and such warmth for the morning's take;
The stock-dove shall hatch her soft brace and shall coo,
While I kiss to the melody, aching all through!

Keats was back at Hampstead by 10 June, when he borrowed a further £30 from the publishers.

Isabella, and the place of their first meeting, was to influence the work of Keats, at least for the next eighteen months – *Endymion* (Book 2), 'Hyperion', 'The Eve of St Agnes' and the fragment of 'The Eve of St Mark'.

In 'Hyperion' (Book 2, lines 300–2), we find a reference that must be to the River Asten, which in the time of Keats turned sharply east to run parallel with the shore until it finally met with the sea at a sluice somewhere near one of the Martello towers. Keats wrote:

> So far her voice flowed on, like timorous brook
> That, lingering along a pebbled coast,
> Doth fear to meet the sea . . .

In the song-poem 'Hush, Hush! Tread Softly!' (stanza one line six) we find another reference to a brook, where he wrote, 'Who dances on bubbles where brooklets meet'.

The 'Hastings Lady', who always seemed an enigma to Keats, was unnamed until about 135 years after his death, when Robert Gittings traced a business letter sent from Hessey to Taylor that identified her as Isabella Jones – a lady well known in their publishing circle. Maybe this explains why she seemed such a mystery, as it suited her to appear enigmatic! The reason she is not mentioned by name in Keats' letters – even those to his brother George, where she is referred to only as the 'Hastings Lady' – is because she wished that she and Keats be acquainted without any of their common acquaintance becoming aware of it. (Her own request to Keats.)

John saw her for a second time a year later, two months before his brother George was to leave for America. They met in the foyer of the Lyceum Theatre in the Strand. Keats was with his own party, George being one of the number. The occasion may have been the stag night before George's wedding to the twenty-year-old Georgiana Wylie. There is no doubt that Keats remembered seeing Isabella, for he mentioned it in a letter to his brother some six or so months later. George had met her before, and they exchanged pleasantries, but as she was with her own party that was as far as it went. She gave no sign that she knew John intimately. Gittings says that they met in the street outside the theatre.

In the first of his long journal letters to George and Georgiana in America, Keats wrote of a new meeting. This letter was written over the period 14–31 October 1818.

> Since I wrote thus far I have met with the same Lady again, whom I saw at Hastings and whom I met when we were going to the English Opera. It was in a street which goes from Bedford Row to Lamb's Conduit Street. – I passed her and turned back: she seemed glad of it – glad to see me, and not offended at my passing her before. We walked on towards Islington, where we called on a friend of hers who keeps a Boarding School. She has always been an enigma to me – she has been in a Room with you and Reynolds, and wishes we should be acquainted without any of our common acquaintance knowing it. As we went along, sometimes through shabby, sometimes through decent Streets, I had my guessing at work, not knowing what it would be, and prepared to meet any surprise. First it ended at this House at Islington: on parting from which I pressed to attend her home. She consented, and then again my thoughts were at work what it might lead to, though now they had received a sort of genteel hint from the Boarding School. Our Walk ended in 34 Gloucester Street, Queen Square – not exactly so, for we went upstairs to her sitting-room, a very tasty sort of place with Books, Pictures, a bronze Statue of Buonaparte, Music, aeolian Harp, a Parrot, a Linnet, a Case of choice Liqueurs, etc. etc. She behaved in the kindest manner – made me take home a Grouse for Tom's dinner. Asked for my address for the purpose of sending more game. – As I had warmed with her before, and kissed her – I though[t] it would be living backwards not to do so again – she had a better taste: she perceived how much a thing of course it was and shrunk from it –

not in a prudish way but in as I say a good taste. She contrived to disappoint me in a way which made me feel more pleasure than a simple Kiss could do – She said I should please her much more if I would only press her hand and go away. Whether she was in a different disposition when I saw her before – or whether I have in fancy wrong'd her I cannot tell. I expect to pass some pleasant hours with her now and then: in which I feel I shall be of service to her in matters of knowledge and taste: if I can I will. I have no Libidinous thought about her [one can only doubt this statement, bearing in mind what had gone before]. She and your George are the only women [of almost my] age whom I would be content to know for their mind and friendship alone. . . .

Robert Gittings said, 'Keats was a normal young man of his time . . .' and we pause to take in this human and delightful picture 'of something that has happened to every young man at one time or another, caught for eternity by Keats's genius and gusto for life'.

Tom died of tuberculosis on 1 December 1818, and in the same month John Keats moved into Wentworth Place to take up lodgings with his friend Charles Brown. Apart from his sister Fanny, who lived with her guardian, Mr Abbey, away over in Walthamstow, Keats had no known relative in England, and Brown was aware of this when he offered Keats the accommodation.

Brown had been invited to spend that Christmas in Chichester, with the parents of his (and also Keats') friend Charles Wentworth Dilke, who shared with Brown the ownership of Wentworth Place. The invitation was extended to Keats, but, being in a distressed and confused state of mind from the recent loss of Tom, Keats put his friend off. However, he promised to follow on later.

It was a whole month before he made the journey. In the meantime he consoled himself with the indulgent Isabella Jones.

Sometime during the months leading up to Tom's death (probably October), he wrote the first version of the sonnet 'Bright Star'. There are conflicting thoughts as to when this was actually written. Joseph Severn found Keats with another version of it on board the *Maria Crowther* during the voyage to Naples in 1820, and he decided (wrongly) that this was the dying spark of his friend's genius. Severn also thought that the sonnet was inspired by his love for Fanny Brawne; but at the time of writing the first version, if it was in October 1818, he had as yet to become seriously involved with her. Was it then inspired by other emotions – emotions that at this time occupied his whole being – those for Isabella?

Biographers and compilers of poetry books claim that the sonnet 'Bright Star' was written in April 1819. Keats gave a copy to Fanny Brawne, who believed it had been written for her. If it was inspired by his infatuation with Isabella, then the sonnet is likely to have been written in the autumn of 1818, for by the April of 1819 he had broken off his relationship with her.

The sonnet appears on page 155 of this book.

Let us return to the walk with Isabella on that visit to her friend at Islington.

The friend was a Mrs Green, the wife of Lieutenant Colonel Thomas Green of the 6th Regiment of Native Infantry, Madras Presidency, who had been invalided out of the army in India after twenty-five years' service. Can this friendship with military people reinforce our theory that the husband of Isabella Jones was an army officer who had been killed in action? What is known does point in this direction, although there is no real proof of such a connection.

Keats had met Fanny Brawne in the October, or early in the November, of 1818. He was close enough to the family to be invited to dine with them at Christmas. He continued his relationship with Isabella, although he was by now attracted to the vivacious Miss Brawne. He describes her in a letter to George as (Chaf and Chat) 'quite outrageous in her behaviour, likely to fly off in all directions', and he named her Millimant.

Keats was not sure of the younger woman, who was much less sophisticated than Isabella and had little interest in poetry or the classics. In fact, the couple were a complete mismatch. Keats wrote to George, 'If I have any more of such behaviour I shall sheer off.' Annoyed, he gave her the copy of 'Bright Star' – not at all gallant! more like the antics of his friend Charles Brown.

The Chichester invitation still stood. The night Keats left for Chichester he stayed in town, planning to catch the early morning coach. (Robert Gittings thought that this was the night of 20 January.) He spent the night with Isabella Jones at her apartment, and we can only surmise what took place within those hours!

At this time, Isabella produced a book of what could be called old wives' tales. Keats was interested in one particular story: the tale of St Agnes Eve.

> Where young virgins might have visions of delight,
> And soft adorings from their loves receive
> Upon the honey'd middle of the night.

In the morning, he boarded the fast coach for Chichester.

With 'Hush, Hush! Tread Softly!' and Isabella's suggestion for a new poem going around in his brain, Keats arrived in Chichester. The city with its twelfth-century cathedral charmed him from his very first view of it. From his perch high up on the outside of the coach, the busy main street stretched before him. He knew at once that his muse waited to fill his receptive mind with poetry. The winter of 1818/19 had been been kind, and the weather for January 1819 was unusually mild, allowing Keats to take a cheaper seat, riding on top of the fast London-to-Chichester coach. As the conveyance rattled through the Northgate, a weak late-afternoon sun bronzed the red-brick buildings.

Charles Brown waited at the travellers' inn in the city centre as Keats' coach pulled up with a clatter of hooves on worn cobbles. Brown immediately noticed his friend's excited state, and his uncommonly fast mode of speech. Keats loved to travel, but his mood went beyond the pleasure he might have received from a mere coach journey. Was there another reason? Could this heightened excitement have had its origins in the previous night's stay at Isabella's apartment?

Keats hardly took a breath from talking as the two friends made their way along East Street to the home of the retired Charles Wentworth Dilke the elder and his wife at 11 The Hornet (Eastgate Square). Built sometime in the 1780s, the tall red-brick house, part of a terrace, retained a look of newness about it. The house, where Keats would spend a few days of his holiday, had been sold at auction in 1813, and it was described in the catalogue as:

> a comfortable dwelling for the retired, with basement, excellent cellarage, ground floor entrance, eating room 17' by 14', a handsome breakfast room, kitchen, scullery, drawing room, bed chambers and attics.

From the guest bedroom in the attic, Keats could look down on the street below, and over the land beyond and the city on either side. The buildings in Eastgate Square still stand today, and, except for conversion to business premises and shops, they are pretty much as they were in Keats' time. High up on the wall of Number 11 a Blue Plaque denotes its use by the poet. The date of his arrival at Chichester comes into question, because in his journal letter to George and his wife in America, which he began writing on 14 February 1819, he wrote:

> since my return from Chichester – I believe I told you I was going thither. I was nearly a fortnight at Mr. John Snook's and a few days at old Mr. Dilke's.

John wrote that he was a few days at old Mr Dilke's, but this does not tally with what is written in some biographies. Robert Gittings, in his book *Keats*, says that Keats arrived in Chichester on 21 January and walked over to Bedhampton on the 23rd. This gives less than two days at Chichester, which can't be right! Andrew Motion in his *Keats* (1997) dates his departure for Sussex as the

18th or 19th of the month; this I feel is the most likely. However, maybe it's safer to say that he left London after the middle of January at a date unknown. He was still in London on the 14th, as he wrote to Benjamin Haydon on that date, although no address or postmark is confirmed for this letter. Some dates are confirmed: Brown and Keats wrote to Maria Dilke from the Mill House at Bedhampton, a joint letter which was dated 24 January – a letter full of fun and puns. Brown states that he and Keats walked over from Chichester on the previous day, which places the walk on the 23rd.

Having left their hosts, the elderly Dilkes, on Saturday the 23rd, Keats and Brown set off to walk the thirteen miles to Bedhampton, where they were to stay with John Snook, the miller, and his wife, Laetitia, sister of Charles Wentworth Dilke, their London friend.

Dark clouds raced over patches of blue sky as the strong south-westerly wind fought off the threatened rain. The fingers of the inlets to Chichester Harbour were white with foam. There was a sparkle to the day, and the two friends were in high spirits as they trudged the unmade road, passing here and there a cottage or two – the homes of fisherfolk and workers of the land. In the open spaces they leant against the strength of the wind, which cut without hindrance across the water. The Mill House and mill were not immediately visible, screened as they were and are today by oak and ash. On the approach the white Mill House stands on the further side of the millstream and a bridge has to be crossed over; a bridge, strong, fashioned with oak timbers from broken-up ships, and built by John Snook's father.

John Snook, a man of ample proportion, met the walkers at his door. As Keats looked upon the smiling face, its skin lined and browned by years of sea winds, he knew that he was going to enjoy his stay. The quietly religious and homely couple lived well in their homely abode, and they were prosperous in their own way. Keats had a room at the back of the house, overlooking the gardens and the estuary beyond.

In a journal letter he wrote to his brother George and his wife 'little George', now in America. The letter was begun on 14 February, after his return to London. He said:

> I went to Chichester and Bedhampton, nothing worth speaking of happened at either place. . . . [If one has enjoyed a quiet restful break, it can often seem as if nothing happened, even when this is not really so.] I was nearly a fortnight at Mr Snook's and a few days at Old Mr Dilke's. I took down some of the thin paper and wrote on it a little poem call'd 'St Agnes Eve' which you shall have as it is, when I have finished the blank part of the rest for you. I went out twice at Chichester to old Dowager card parties, I see very little now, and very few Persons – being almost tired of men and things.

His 'old black dog' began to haunt him again soon after his return to Hampstead. The few happy, carefree days at Bedhampton were in the past.

> I said nothing of consequence passed at Snook's – no more than this – that I like the family very much. . . .
> The only time I went out from Bedhampton was to see a chapel consecrated – Brown, I and John Snook the boy, went in a chaise behind a leaden horse. Brown drove, but the horse did not mind him. This Chapel is built by a Mr. Way, a great Jew converter, who in that line has spent one hundred thousand pounds. He maintains a great number of poor Jews – *Of course his communion plate was stolen*. He spoke to the clerk about it – The clerk said he was very sorry, adding, *"I dare shay, your honour, it's among ush."*
> The chapel is built in Mr. Way's park. The consecration was not amusing. There were numbers of carriages – and his house crammed with clergy – they sanctified the Chapel, and it being a wet day, consecrated the burial-ground through the vestry window. I begin to hate parsons; they did not make me love them that day when I saw them in their proper colours.

With Keats' feelings as they were on the Church and clergy, it seems strange that he agreed to go. Religious ceremonies were not events that he normally went to. His going at all was no doubt due to the reputation of the great Stansted House and Stansted Park. The advertisement for the event in the *Hampshire Telegraph* went thus:

Stansted Chapel

> The Consecration of the Chapel in Stansted Park will take place on Monday the 25th instant. (being the Holyday of the Conversion of St Paul). Notice is hereby given, that the Doors will be shut, and the Chapel kept empty 'till the commencement of the Service, when no one will be admitted within the Walls without a ticket. As it is requisite that the Clergy should appear in their Canonicals a Room will be provided for their accommodation.

Whether or not they had tickets, early on the morning of 25 January the friends set out for Stansted Park accompanied by the Snooks' young son, another John. The distance from the Mill House to Stansted Park is five miles. The horse drawing their open trap was stubborn, every so often lowering its head to eat the roadside grass. The head could not be pulled up by the reins, and, to get the beast to move, someone had to alight and pull against the bit harness. This task fell to the young Snook. Keats wrote, 'Brown drove, but the horse did not mind him.' In fact, better progress could have been made on foot.

The weather didn't improve Brown's temper. Every so often a strong gust of wind, carrying stinging rain, screeched in from the harbour. Keats' throat, which had improved during the days at Chichester, began to tighten.

They arrived late, as a little sun found its way through the racing cloud. The chapel was jammed full with a hundred more people than it could comfortably accommodate. Clergy and gentry stifled together. Keats and Brown could not get beyond the draughty porch, and, in spite of pleas to let the boy through, they were forced to stay where they where, unable to move back or forward. The service was conducted by two of the leading churchmen of the day, but their rank and importance would have had little effect on John, stuck as he was in his position near the porch door with the cold wind dragging at his turned-up collar. Although his ears were shut, his eyes were open. He took in the coloured glass windows – especially the one designed by Lewis Way, depicting the Jewish candelabra and the escutcheon of the Fitzalan family.

Keats probably spent two hours at the chapel and another hour at the great house. The house and chapel both feature in his poem 'The Eve of St Agnes':

> A Casement tripple arch'd and diamonded
> With many coloured glass fronted the Moon
> In midst where of a shielded scutcheon shed
> High blushing gules; and She kneeled saintly down
> And inly prayed for grace and heavenly boon;
> The blood red gules fell on her silver cross
> And her white hands devout.

This is taken from the manuscript reproduced in The Wordsworth Poetry Library: *The Works of John Keats*. The published version follows the poems and verses of John Keats by John Middleton Murry:

> A casement high and triple-arch'd there was,
> All garlanded with craven imag'ries
> Of fruits, and flowers, and bunches of knot-grass,
> And diamonded with panes of quaint device,
> Innumerable of stains and splendid dyes,
> As are the tiger-moth's deep-damask'd wings.
> And in the midst, 'mong thousand heraldries,
> And twilight saints, and dim emblazonings,
> A shielded scutcheon blush'd with blood of queens and kings.

Keats returned to the Mill House, his throat raging. The only good thing about the journey back was the swiftness of the horse homeward bound. Laetitia Snook made a hot broth and bundled him to bed, where he stayed the next day, saying goodbye to Brown, who was returning to Hampstead, from beneath the sheets.

Two days later, in the Snooks' copy of the *Hampshire Telegraph*, he read an account of the occasion, including the banquet at the house following the chapel consecration; the fare had been 'sumptuous'.

In the peace of the bedroom at the back of the Mill House he worked steadily on the 'St Agnes Eve' manuscript; he wrote and changed, changed and crossed through. The wind, though easing, was still strong enough to rattle the windows with sleety rain. Even had he been well, it was not weather to walk out in. That he felt chilled comes through in stanza 1:

> St Agnes' Eve – Ah, bitter chill it was!
> The owl, for all his feathers, was a-cold;
> The hare limp'd trembling through the frozen grass,
> And silent was the flock in woolly fold;
> Numb were the Beadsman's fingers, while he told
> His rosary, and while his frosted breath,
> Like pious incense from a censer old,
> Seem'd taking flight for heaven, without a death,
> Past the Virgin's picture, while his prayer he saith.

Although the frost had not arrived, heavy snowstorms were just three weeks away. As he vacated the comfortable room, and said his goodbyes to the kindly Snooks, he could not have known that his very last night in England would be spent in that same room twenty months later.

All through the St Agnes Eve poem the influence of the cathedral and buildings in Chichester, the great house at Stansted and Way's chapel can be found.

In stanza 2 we are inside the cathedral:

> His prayer he saith, this patient, holy man;
> Then takes his lamp, and riseth from his knees,
> And back returneth, meagre, barefoot, wan,
> Along the chapel aisle by slow degrees:
> The sculptur'd dead on each side seem to freeze,
> Emprison'd in black, purgatorial rails:
> Knights, ladies, praying in dumb orat'ries,
> He passeth by; and his weak spirit fails
> To think how they may ache in icy hoods and mails.

In stanza 6 Keats tells the story of the legend:

> They told how, upon St Agnes' Eve,
> Young virgins might have visions of delight,
> And soft adorings from their loves receive
> Upon the honey'd middle of the night,
> If ceremonies due they did aright;
> As, supperless to bed they must retire,
> And couch supine their beauties, lily white;
> Nor look behind, nor sideways, but require
> Of Heaven with upward eyes for all that they desire.

In stanza 12, with the conversation between Porphyro and old Angela, the poet takes us back to the situation at Bo-Peep, Hastings, and the 'irascible' old Donat O'Callaghan:

> "Get hence! get hence! there's dwarfish Hildebrand;
> "He had a fever late, and in the fit
> "He cursed thee and thine, both house and land:
> "Then there's that old Lord Maurice, not a whit
> "More tame for his grey hairs – Alas me! flit!
> "Flit like a ghost away". – Ah gossip dear,
> "We're safe enough; here in this arm-chair sit,
> "And tell me how" – Good saints! not here, Not here;
> "Follow me child, or else these stones will be thy bier.

In stanza 38 there are definite connotations of sexual gratification; in the original manuscript these feelings were more explicitly expressed, leading to an argument with Taylor and Hessey, who believed that the stanza would offend female readers. Keats, angry, replied that he 'would consider any man a Eunuch, who would leave a maid of that disposition in such a way'.

> "My Madeline! sweet dreamer! lovely bride!
> Say, may I be for aye thy vassal blest?
> Thy beauty's shield, heart-shap'd and vermeil dyed?
> Ah silver shrine, here will I take my rest
> After so many hours of toil and quest,
> A famish'd pilgrim, – sav'd by miracle.
> Though I have found, I will not rob thy nest
> Saving of thy sweet self; if thou think'st well
> to trust, fair Madeline, to no rude infidel."

Taylor thought that this would go against the poem, as it gave the feeling that the love affair was consummated. In his poem is Keats hinting that during the night stay with Isabella, before leaving for Chichester, he had consummated his own love affair? If he had, could this then explain his state of excitement during the first days of his stay in Chichester?

By 4 February 1819 he was back at Hampstead. On the 13th, a Saturday, he was in town. He made several calls, and, although he does not record it, he visited Isabella Jones. In her rooms he read over the rough manuscript of 'St Agnes Eve'. She seems to have been delighted with the work, and she suggested another topic for a poem. On his return that night to Hampstead, inspired by Isabella he began to write 'The Eve of St Mark'. The legend of St Mark's Eve is that:

> Any that stand on the night of the 24th of April, St Marks Eve, at the Church Yard gate for three years in succession will at the hour of twelve upon the night, see in visions the phantasm of all who will die in the year to come.

Many have puzzled as to why the poem was never finished. Why towards the end of that February did he stop writing in mid-sentence, with the words 'at Venice'? John never mentions the poem or Isabella Jones after this time.

Robert Gittings, in his *Keats*, says that stanza 4 of 'The Eve of St Mark' is almost a description of Isabella's room.

> All was silent, all was gloom,
> Abroad and in the homely room:
> Down she sat, poor cheated soul!
> And struck a lamp from the dismal coal;
> Lean'd forward, with bright drooping hair
> And slant book, full against the glare.
> Her shadow, in uneasy guise,
> Hover'd about, a giant size,
> On ceiling-beam and old oak chair,
> The parrot's cage, and panel square;
> And the warm angled winter screen,
> On which were many monsters seen,
> Call'd doves of Siam, Lima mice,
> And legless birds of Paradise,
> Macaw, and tender Avadavat,
> And silken-furr'd Angora cat.
> Untir'd she read, her shadow still
> Glower'd about, as it would fill
> The room with wildest forms and shades,
> As though some ghostly queen of spades
> Had come to mock behind her back,
> And dance, and ruffle her garments black.

On 24 February, Keats found himself caught in a snowstorm whilst in town. He stayed for two nights with Taylor in Fleet Street. It seems likely that something occurred during this time to alter his relationship with Isabella, for, although he had intended to go on with his visits to her, he never mentioned her again for the rest of his life. The most likely explanation for this is that, during the two nights at Taylor's, he found that she was also romantically involved with his publisher. John hated any dishonest situation; maybe he sensed that he was being played with. Several resentful phases in his letters of the following months suggest that he had been badly treated by a woman. No woman of his acquaintance fits except Isabella. The letters between Taylor and Isabella Jones that have survived reveal more than a trace of sexual banter, and it's possible that by this time she had become his mistress. We note that John Taylor was unlucky in love and remained a lifetime bachelor. The reason for Isabella's request that they should see each other 'without any of [their] common acquaintance knowing it' now became clear to the poet. This may be why Keats stopped work on 'The Eve of St Mark', putting down his pen in mid-sentence.

He put away the fragment and did not touch it again until seven months later, when he sent a copy of it to his brother George.

The enforced secrecy of his relationship with Isabella must have irked a man of Keats' outgoing nature. Also, he had been seeing Fanny Brawne at the same time, and maybe felt that he himself was acting in a dishonest manner.

John fell into one of his long periods of depression. Haydon suggests that at this time he began to drink heavily, although Charles Cowden Clarke disputes Haydon's account of the poet's behaviour.

Whatever Isabella Jones' character, we cannot take her from the life of Keats without giving credit to her for the inspiration of at least one of his great poems.

John Taylor, the publisher, wrote poetry, some of which he published. Most of his poetry was on events in his daily life or religion, for he was a deeply religious man, but in 1819 his rather dull sonnets revealed a brooding passion. One written in the January tells of a series of encouragements and rebuffs, such as Keats had complained of in 'You Say You Love'. In a later sonnet, Taylor uses the name Isabel; this, then, must be the same Isabella, unless Taylor, lucky or unlucky, knew two attractive women with the same name.

Very little is known of Mrs Jones from then on. A letter survives, written to Taylor in May of the same year, in which she hints at poor health. In the early spring she became unwell and left town – not for Hastings and Bo-Peep, but for Tunbridge Wells to take the cure there.

Her letter goes:

> You once favoured me with the most amusing and delightful letter I ever read, (Love epistles excepted) and at a time when perhaps I did not feel its value; being then blest with better health; now I request that you will in charity write . . .

She sat for her portrait by the painter A. E. Chalon sometime in the winter of 1818. This portrait appeared in the Royal Academy Exhibition of 1819, along with Joseph Severn's miniature of Keats. John, going to view his own portrait, may possibly have seen hers. Isabella's portrait painting has been lost to us.

Here are some extracts from letters that Isabella wrote to John Taylor (she had moved from 34 Gloucester Street, Queens Square):

> 57 Lamb's Conduit Street, Mr John Taylor
> [Probably written late 1819.]
>
> My dear Sir,
>
> I most sincerely and selfishly hope that you are recovered from your late indisposition [Taylor had been ill that year], because I now claim your promise of assisting at my House Warming, which takes place Wednesday next – you shall have pretty women to look at – sensible men to talk with – the cosiest corner in the room – a tass of real Farentosh [expensive Scotch whisky] and last but not least a hearty welcome from my dear Sir [probably Donat O'Callaghan].
>
> Yours very truly,
> Isabella Jones

And again another invitation, which was maybe a year later:

57 Lamb's Conduit Street, Mr John Taylor

My dear Sir,
　Will you favour me with your agreeable society on Friday evening next, and persuade Mr Reynolds to accompany you? I will not bribe you with a Bill of Fare as I did last year, but will regard your accepting this invitation as a proof that you have not entirely forgotten,
　　Tea at 7 o'clock.
　　Yours very truly
　　　Isabella Jones

After Keats' death, Taylor seems to have passed to Mrs Jones letters written to him by Joseph Severn, relating to the events that led up to Keats' demise.

She returned the letters with one of her own describing her feelings, which are not those one would expect from one on the death of a friend and possible lover. There are no postmarks, but the date of writing seems to be 14 April 1821.

　To John Taylor Esq.

My dear Sir,
　I return the letters with many thanks for your kind indulgence. I began to read them, with a heartfelt interest – a favourable impression towards the author and with feelings well calculated to fulfil your prediction – "That I should be much affected" – What will you say when I confess that I am greatly disappointed – that I could not shed a single tear – and that I do not like Mr Severn. I never saw so much egotism and selfishness displayed under the mask of feeling and friendship – I got through the first letter, pretty well; I did not like his flood of tears "en parenthese", as Mr Maturin would say [Robert C. Maturin (1782–1824), novelist], or his liberal remark upon the Captain of the Ship. I took up the second, expecting to meet with some account of the interesting invalid without interruption from the Lady's fits [Miss Cotterell, a fellow consumptive passenger aboard the *Maria*

Crowther], but no – the cloven foot, appeared again – the eternal I – I – like Aaron's serpent swallowed up all proper feeling and I threw the letter from me, with the painful impression in my mind, that the fine hearted we both admired died in horror – no kind hope to smooth his pillow – no philosophy – no religion to support him! There follows a sentiment a La John Bunyan about "Angels of Goodness" and "Dark wilderness" – Where was Mr Severn's religion at this trying moment? Oh – he was like the Pharisee in the Temple, thanking God for the modicum he possessed!!! Instead of copying Raphael, I should advise his painting the Good Samaritan – My temper and patience "broke down under the trial". Of the third letter, which I will not comment on, or you will think me the veriest shrew alive – Of all the cants, in this canting world the cant of sentiment is the most disgusting, and I never saw better specimens than these letters afford – they are extremely well got up and will impose upon the most literate – but do let me flatter myself that, we carry a test in the true feeling of our hearts, that exposes all such hollow pretensions – His own letter to Mr Brown with all its quaintness and harmless conceit is worth a wagon load of Mr Egotist's productions [Keats to Brown from Rome, 30 November 1820 – this shows that Isabella had seen one of Keats' most intimate letters and knew about his feelings toward Fanny Brawne]. When I have the pleasure of seeing you – we will compare notes upon this subject – my mind is always open to conviction and I have been so often flattered by observing a coincidence of ideas between us, and have so high an opinion of your judgement, that I lose confidence in myself when I differ from you – I have not forgotten the Knife, but must receive the "penny fee" myself or the charm will be broken [it being considered unlucky to give a cutting instrument to a friend or lover, because the relationship will be cut, therefore the receiver must pay some small coinage for the item]. I send a Banquet in a classical jug for your Mantle shelf – you will require some sweets to qualify, the bitterness of this angry letter – pray pardon me, I sat down to the task, with a mind prepared to sympathise with all poor Keats' sufferings, and ones best feelings are checked by an elaborate account of sweeping rooms – making beds and blowing fires! I feel a relapse taking place – my ears tingle – my pen shakes – I shall be a stiffened corpse if I do not conclude – God bless you dear Mr Taylor and make you as happy as I wish you. Remember me to Mr Hessey.

    Ever yours very truly
      Isabella Jones

Poor Severn! Poor Severn indeed! What a shameful reflection on his diligent care of the dying poet! Keats may have turned in his new grave if he had known that the woman who had, so he believed, wronged him, was reading letters that certainly were not meant for her eyes.

Little is known about the life of Mrs Jones; there is no record of her birth or death. She definitely had a connection with the Whig family O'Callaghan, and that she had Whig sympathies is born out by the bust of Buonaparte that Keats saw in her apartment. It's possible that she was one of the many Whig hostesses of the Regency period. She does seem to have had an unsettled lifestyle, moving from one furnished apartment to another over short periods: 34 Gloucester Street; 57 Lamb's Conduit Street; Clifden House, Tunbridge Wells; and summer months spent at Bo-Peep, Hastings.

Frances Brawne (Fanny)

Fanny, the first child of Samuel and Frances Brawne, was born on 9 August 1800. The Brawnes lived at the time on a farm in the hamlet of West End.

Fanny's father, Samuel, died whilst she was a young girl, but not before the family had increased by two more: a boy, Samuel, and another girl, Margaret. The Brawnes were not well off. Although Samuel Brawne is recorded as being of independent means, he is not said to have been a farmer.

After the death of her husband, Mrs Brawne suffered reduced circumstances until a relation of her husband's died, leaving the little family a legacy to ease their situation. When Charles Brown and Keats went on their walking tour of the North and Scotland in July 1818, Brown, as was his custom, rented out his part of Wentworth Place. The tenant for that summer was Mrs Brawne.

When Keats returned to London early because of his poor health, he went directly to Wentworth Place to see the Dilkes. Maria Dilke describes his wild appearance in a letter to her father-in-law at Chichester dated 19 August 1818:

> John Keats arrived here last night, as brown and as shabby as you can imagine, scarcely any shoes left, his jacket all torn at the back, a fur cap, a great plaid, and his knapsack, I cannot tell what he looked like.

The Brawnes next door may have seen his arrival, but, as he stayed for a very short time only, it's unlikely.

Keats, alarmed to hear that his brother Tom's health was now in a dangerous state, rushed to the lodging that they shared at Bentley's house in Well Walk. He found Tom spitting blood.

Mrs Bentley, the postman's wife, who had cared for Tom Keats whilst his brother John was on the Scottish tour, is described by Dilke as a 'well behaved, kind and motherly person'. It would have been this, and the proximity of his friends the Dilkes, that made it possible for Keats to leave his brother alone at the start of his walk.

Charles Wentworth Dilke recorded: 'Keats met Miss Brawne at my house about October or November 1818.' He also said her brother Samuel was at the time still in education, and that Margaret was a child.

Another member of the Brawne household at the time was Carlo, Mrs Brawne's mongrel dog.

Fanny Brawne was eighteen years of age when she came into Keats' life. The story of their love and time together will appear as we look into the letters Keats wrote to her.

Most of Keats' friends deplored the association; they disliked Fanny to an extreme. These people guarded their friendship with the poet jealously. The Dilke family, however, were friendly and supportive even in her later life, with one exception: Dilke's grandson Sir Charles Wentworth hated her with a passion. For reasons known only to himself, he collected together all of her letters to the poet that he could find, and later burnt them in the fireplace of his parlour.

John and Fanny became secretly engaged early in 1819. Her mother must have viewed the matter with some trepidation, for her daughter's betrothed had poor prospects, and he was in the first stages of a serious illness.

Fanny is shown to be a lively personality, with a love of dancing and social occasions. She was a skilled dressmaker and made clothes to supplement family finances. She had some literary skill, spoke fluent French, and had a working knowledge of German. A German story called 'Nickel List and his Merry Men', translated into English by her, was seen by Maurice Buxton Foreman (a Keats biographer).

Fanny's brother Samuel died with tuberculosis as a young man in 1828; her sister Margaret survived to live a long life.

When Brown returned to Hampstead in September 1818, Mrs Brawne moved her family to another address: Elm Cottage, near the top of Downshire Hill, Hampstead. The cottage was advertised in *The Times* on 19 March 1822:

> 'Small detached cottage' Hampstead, to be let – at West End Hampstead 'Elm Cottage' on a repairing lease of 8 years – at a low rent. Containing 2 sitting rooms, 2 bedrooms, 5 small ditto – kitchen, wash-house &c and neat garden.

In March 1819 Dilke moved from Hampstead to Westminster for his son Charlie's education, and the Brawnes moved back to Wentworth Place, where they rented the Dilkes' half of the property.

Tom Keats died on 1 December 1818, and John moved in to lodge with his friend Brown. Fanny was living next door, with just a wall between them. The happenings over the next twelve months are revealed in the letters which they wrote to each other.

When Keats died far away in Italy, Fanny was still resident at Wentworth Place. She was just twenty years old. She went into deep mourning, and remained a spinster for the next twelve years.

On 26 November, on a dark and windy night in 1829, Mrs Brawne, Fanny's mother, was showing a guest to the door of Wentworth Place when a gust of wind directed the flame of the candle that she was carrying on to the ruff of her sleeve. The flame quickly spread to the front of her dress, and before help could arrive she was badly burned. A few hours later she died of her injuries. She was buried at St Martin-in-the-Fields on 1 December 1829.

At the age of thirty-three, on 15 June 1833, at the parish church of St Marylebone, Fanny married a Spanish gentleman eleven years her junior – Louis Lindo. On the marriage certificate, his name was changed to Lindon.

During the Great Exhibition of 1851, Louis was appointed Secretary to the Exhibition by Sir Charles Dilke, the son of Dilke.

Fanny died on 4 December 1865, and her husband followed her on 21 October 1872. Both lie in the same grave in Brompton Cemetery, London.

A friend of Fanny Keats' husband, Valentin Llanos, met Fanny Brawne soon after the poet's death. Describing her, he wrote:

> I am greatly interested in the family, Keats you must know was in love, and the lady whom he was to have married, had he survived, attended him to the last. [Of course this was not quite so.] She is a beautiful young creature, but now wasted away to a skeleton, and will follow him shortly, I believe. She and her sister say they often found Keats on entering a room, with the Blackwoods review in his hand, reading as if he would devour it. The instant he observed anybody near him however, he would throw it by, and begin to talk of some indifferent matter.

Blackwood's Edinburgh Magazine had attacked and insulted Keats and his poems in 1817, but it's unlikely that Keats was that much troubled by it.

On another occasion Llanos wrote:

> I met miss Brawne, of whom I spoke to you some time since – sadly changed and worn, I thought, but still most animated, lively and even witty in conversation. She quite dazzled me in spite of her pale looks. Her sister was there, younger and prettier, but not so clever.

In December 1829, eight years after the poet's death, Fanny received a letter from Charles Brown, who at the time was living in Italy. He, unaware of her circumstances and her mother's recent ghastly death, wrote in all ignorance what must have seemed to the recipient a harassing letter:

Miss Brawne, Wentworth Place, Hampstead.
Florence. 17th December 1829.

My dear Miss Brawne,

Without any apology for our long silence, let me hope you are in the best health, that your mother is better, and that Margaret is never ailing; to which I add a merry Xmas and a happy new year to all. Now, with these good wishes, I may begin. A few days ago, I received a letter from the Galignani in Paris telling me they are on the eve of publishing the works of Keats, and asking for his autograph. I sent it to them, with a letter stating it was always my intention to write his life, and annex it to a Tragedy of his, together with some unpublished poems in my possession, whenever his countrymen should have learnt to value his poetry. I also told them I believed that time was arrived, as needs it must, sooner or later; but that I was fearful it was too late for me to enter into any arrangement with them. Whatever their answer may be, I am resolved to write his life, persuaded that no one, except yourself, knew him better. Leigh Hunt's account of him is worse than disappointing; I cannot bear it; it seems as if Hunt was so impressed by his illness, that he had utterly forgotten him in health. This is a dreadful mistake, because it is our duty to his memory to show the ruin his enemies had effected; and I will not spare them. It is not my present purpose to enter into any criticism on his works, but to let it be simply a biography; and, to make that as vivid as possible, I shall incorporate into it passages from letters to me, and to his brothers, – which last are in my possession; together with passages from particular poems, or entire ones, relating to himself, always avoiding those which regard you, unless you let me know that I may, without mentioning your name, introduce them. There are, however two of his letters which I wish to give entire; one written when he despaired of Tom's recovery, the other when he despaired of his own. This latter one is of the most painful description; therefore I wish it to be known, that Gifford and Lockhart may be thoroughly hated and despised. The question is whether you will object to it; I think you will not. Though much of it regards you, your name is never once mentioned. Then again, those poems addressed to you, which you permitted me to copy, – may I publish them? It is impossible for me to judge of your feelings on the subject; but whatever they are, you are certain that I shall obey them. To my mind you ought to consent, as no greater honour can be paid to a woman than to be beloved by such a man as Keats. I am aware that, at a more recent period, you would have been startled at its being alluded to; but consider that eight years have passed away; and now, no one, if you do not, can object to it. Besides, Hunt has alluded to you, and what more will it be to give his poems addressed to that lady? Your name will still remain as secret to the world as before. I shall of course scrupulously avoid intimating who you are, or in what part of England you reside. As his love for you formed so great a part of him, we may be doing him an injustice in being silent on it: Indeed something must be said especially as Hunt has said something. We live among strange customs; for had you been husband and wife, though but for an hour, everyone would have thought himself at liberty publicly to speak of, and all about you; but as you were only so in your hearts, it seems, as it were, improper. Think of it in your best train for thinking, my dear Miss Brawne, and let me know your decision. I have turned it in my mind a great deal, and find nothing, to confess the truth freely, – against it. Three months ago I heard you were at Bruges, on a visit to your aunt; but I suppose you are, by this time returned. Give my kindest remembrances to Mrs Brawne and Margaret. [As said, Brown had no knowledge of Mrs Brawne's so recent death.] Carlino and I lead very comfortable, happy, healthy lives, with short lessons, long walks, and, now and then, a game at romps, or "ballo grande" at the Opera.

    Believe me always.
       Yours most sincerely,
         Cha's Brown

That Fanny sat down to answer Brown's letter almost at once shows a depth of character beyond what could have been expected in her disturbed circumstance, having buried her mother just three weeks before.

    The letter that we have has been termed a draft copy; certainly it is full of mistakes and crossings-out. We make no attempt to replicate these errors and crossings-out here, but put the gist of the letter together as best we may.

29 December 1829. Hampstead.

My dear Mr Brown,

As the aggressor I am too happy to escape the apologies I owe you on my long silence, not gladly to take your hint and say nothing about it, the best reparation I can make is to answer your letter of today as soon as possible, although I received it only this morning; in the hours that have intervened before I sat down to answer it, my feelings have entirely changed on the subject of the request it contains. Perhaps you will think I was opposed to it, and am now come over to your side of the question, but it is just the contrary. Had I answered your letter immediately I should have told you that I considered myself so entirely unconnected with Mr Keats, except for my own feelings, that nothing published respecting him could affect me, but now I see it differently. We have all our little world in which we figure and I cannot help expressing some disinclination that the few acquaintances I have should be able to obtain such a key to my sensations. Having said so much you will probably conclude that I mean to refuse your request. Perhaps when I assure you that though my opinion has changed, my intention of complying in every respect with your wishes remains, you will think I am mentioning my objections to make a favour of my consent, but indeed my dear Mr Brown if you do, you mistake me entirely. It is only to justify myself I own, that I state all I think to you. I am very grateful, nor ought I have gone so far without thanking you for your kindness and consideration in writing to me on the subject. I assure you I should not have hinted that your wishes were painful to me did I not feel the suffering myself to be even alluded to was a want of pride. So far am I from possessing overstrained delicacy, that the circumstance of its being a mere love story is the least of my concern; on the contrary, had I been his wife I should have felt my present reluctance would have been so much stronger that I think I must have made it my request that you would relinquish your intention. The only thing that saves me now, is that so few can know I am in any way implicated, and that of those few, I may hope the greater number may never see the book in Question.

Do then entirely as you please, and be assured that I comply with your wishes, rather because they are yours, than with the expectation of any good that can be done. I fear the kindest act would be to let him rest for ever in the obscurity to which unhappy circumstance have condemned him. [Fanny cannot have known just how wrong she was in making this statement.] Will the writings that remain of his rescue him from it? You can tell better than I, and are more impartial on the subject, my wish has long been that his name, his very name could be forgotten by every one but myself, that I have often wished most intensely.

To your publishing his poems addressed to me, I do not see there can be any objection after the subject has been once alluded to, if you think them worthy of him.

I entirely agree with you that if his life is to be published no part ought to be kept back, for all you can show is his character, his life was too short and too unfortunate for any thing else. I have no doubt that his talents would have been great, not the less for their being developed rather late which I believe was the case; all I fear is whether he has left enough to make people believe that.

If I could think so, I should consider it right to make that sacrifice to his reputation that I now do to your kind motives. Not that even the establishment of his fame would give me the pleasure it ought. Without claiming too much constancy for myself I may truly say that he is well remembered by me, and that satisfied with that I could wish no one but myself knew he had ever existed, but I confess as he was so much calumniated and suffered so much from it, it is perhaps the duty of those who loved and valued him to vindicate him also, and if it can be done, all the friends that time has left him, and I above all must be deeply indebted to you. I am glad you feel that Mr Hunt gave him a weakness of character that surely only belonged to his ill health. Mr Hazlitt, if I remember rightly in his remarks used five or six years ago is still more positive in fixing it on him. I should be glad if you could disprove I was a very poor judge of character ten years ago, and probably overrated every good quality he had, but surely they go to far on the other side; after all he was but four and twenty when his illness began and he had gone through a great deal of vexation before.

Here the letter ends. There is no signature, so it is possible that some part is missing. The letter was addressed to 'Signor Charles Brown. Gentiluomo Inglesi. Firenze. Italia'.

In a letter to Fanny Keats, the poet's sister, on 18 September 1820, after Keats had left London for Italy, Fanny Brawne wrote about Keats' numerous devoted friends:

I am certain he has some spell that attaches them to him, or else he has fortunately met with a set of friends that I did not believe could be found in the world.

Dilke claimed that Keats met Fanny Brawne in November at his house, Wentworth Place, Hampstead. Charles Dilke is regarded as a trustworthy recorder of the time, and there is no reason to doubt his account. Fanny was eighteen and a quarter at the time of their meeting, but she looked younger. Keats and Fanny were the firstborn children of their respective families, and they both suffered the deaths of their fathers during their childhoods. Thomas Keats and Samuel Brawne had both died in their thirties: Keats was killed in a fall from his horse, and Brawne died of consumption. Both men had family connections to horses and coaching, as *their* fathers had both earned a living as 'stable keepers'. Keats was an orphan, his mother having succumbed to the scourge of the age: tuberculosis. Fanny's mother, Frances Brawne, after whom she was named, still lived, a widow of forty-seven. Mrs Brawne looked younger than her true age, and both had the same facial features. Mrs Brawne had married a man younger than herself, and Fanny eventually followed in her mother's footsteps, marrying a man eleven years her junior.

Fanny could not be considered a beauty, but she was unusual and attractive. She had a pale complexion, warm-brown hair and bright blue eyes. Someone who knew her described her as 'at once attracting attention', she was vivacious and animated in company and has been described as a dazzling personality. Her skill at dressmaking supplemented the family's income, helping them through their many ups and downs. She made dresses for herself and her sister – dresses that were fashionable for their time. It's very likely that she also took paid commissions from outside the family circle. She enjoyed the theatre, dancing and social engagements. She seems not to have been a great reader, except for the cheap novels of the day. She enjoyed them, but she laughed at herself for wasting her hours on such rubbish. Fanny had little interest in poetry, except for the works of Byron (not a favourite of Keats') and Shakespeare.

Keats said that she was not attracted to him for his poetry, and she admitted that she did not understand it. The only poetry that we know that she wrote is a couplet written in French when she was still a schoolgirl. French was a language in which she had a fluency not shared by Keats, who had no understanding of the spoken French language.

In a letter to his brother George, now in America, Keats wrote:

> Shall I give you Miss Brawne? She is about my height [a little over five foot] – with a fine style of countenance of the lengthened sort – she wants sentiment in every feature – she manages to make her hair look well – her nostrils are fine – though a little painful – her mouth is bad and good – her Profile is better than her full-face which indeed is not full but pale and thin without showing any bone. Her shape is very graceful and so are her movements – her Arms are good her hands baddish – her feet tolerable. She is not seventeen [Keats mistakes her age] – but she is ignorant – monstrous in her behaviour, flying out in all directions – calling people such names that I was forced lately to make use of the term *Minx* – this is I think not from any innate vice, but from a penchant she has for acting stylishly – I am however tired of such style and shall decline any more of it.

Keats wrote this after knowing Fanny for just six months. He is interested enough to reveal to his brother the virtues and faults of this young woman to whom he is becoming enamoured.

Of him she said:

> His conversation was in the highest degree interesting and his spirits good, excepting at moments when anxiety regarding his brother's health dejected them.

Tom was very ill, and just a month away from death. In the letter to George, John also wrote:

> Mrs. Brawne who took Brown's house for the Summer, still resides in Hampstead. She is a very nice woman, and her daughter senior is I think beautiful and elegant, graceful, silly, fashionable, and strange. We have a little tiff now and then – and she behaves a little better, or I must have sheered off.

Fanny was very young and she was petite – attributes which were, to a man of his short stature and ideals, very attractive. There was something in his make-up that preferred a lack of maturity in women. Taller women made him self-conscious about his own height, for he was not more than an inch over five foot. He disliked dancing for the same reason, saying that he felt ridiculous when dancing with a tall girl.

Isabella Jones, whom he was also seeing at this time, was cultured and self-assured – a women of the world – and, although she excited him, it was a different feeling to the one he was experiencing with his new interest, Fanny. He was not in complete control with Isabella; she evidently puzzled him, and she remained an enigma.

Fanny Brawne's extravagant behaviour was a sign that she was far from self-assured and was trying to overcome her immaturity. No letters from her to the poet survive, but what can be read into his own letters to her indicates that hers were ingenuous and conventional. There seems to be no similarity between the letters that Fanny wrote and those of Isabella that have survived.

Keats, though not comfortable in the company of women, was prone to fall in love easily. One might say that he fell in love with love itself. He once claimed, "Even a bit of ribbon was a matter of interest to me." Did he fall for Fanny on first sight? Men have a penchant for telling women that they have, and John Keats was no exception. Later he told her, "The very first week I knew you I wrote myself your vassal, but burnt the Letter as the very next time I thought you manifested some dislike to me."

By the middle of December, Keats began to tire of Fanny's manner. He had written little for months. For one reason or another, poetry had gone by the board. Bentley, his former landlord, arrived at Wentworth Place with a clothes basket filled with books from his Well Walk lodgings. Their arrival spurred him to get on with some serious work. He said, "I live under an everlasting restraint – never relieved except when I am composing – so I will write away."

An invitation from the elderly Dilkes for Brown and Keats to stay with them at Chichester was still outstanding, but John's mind was in turmoil. He had recently buried his brother Tom. His grief, however, was relieved a little by the attentions of Fanny.

Mrs Brawne invited him to spend Christmas Day with them at Elm Cottage, which he accepted although it seems he had an understanding with Mrs Reynolds and her family that he would dine with them on the same day. The Reynolds family, mother and daughters, already hated Fanny Brawne and this was the last straw! John was forced to write a difficult letter of apology:

> December 1818.
> Little Britain, Christ's Hospital.
>
> My dear Mrs. Reynolds –
> When I left you yesterday, 'twas with the conviction that you thought I had received no previous invitation for Christmas day: the truth is I had, and had accepted it under the conviction that I should be in Hampshire at the time: else believe me I should not have done so, but kept in Mind my old friends. I will not speak of the proportion of pleasure I may receive at different Houses –

that never enters my head – you may take for a truth that I would have given up even what I did see to be a greater pleasure, for the sake of old acquaintanceship – time is nothing – two years are as long as twenty.
   Yours faithfully
   John Keats

There is no doubt that the day he spent with Fanny would have been the greater pleasure!

With Brown already in Chichester, Keats was spending a deal of time with the Dilkes next door. He dined with them after Christmas on game birds given him by Isabella Jones. Maria Dilke wrote to her parents-in-law with a warning of what to expect on the arrival of John at Chichester: 'You will find him a very odd young man, but good tempered and very clever indeed.'

Keats made two fruitless trips into the city during January: one to persuade his sister's guardian, Abbey, to keep up her schooling, and the other to the same gentleman in an effort to borrow money for Benjamin Haydon.

Abbey accused Keats of being a troublemaker as regards his sister Fanny's affairs, and he said he wished that John would cease corresponding with her. As to the matter of money for Haydon, he refused the request point-blank. He told Keats that there was little enough in the account for his own needs.

After the first flush of excitement had abated, Keats' declared love seems to have turned to resentment; he was disturbed at the way his attraction to Fanny had affected his mind, and began a strange resentment against her for stealing away his freedom. It's likely that he further upset Fanny with his remarkable rudeness to one of her friends. He wrote about it in the long letter to his brother George:

> She had a friend to visit her lately – you have known plenty such – her face is raw as if she was standing out in a frost; her lips raw and seem always ready for a Pullet – she plays the Music without one sensation but the feel of the ivory at her fingers. She is a downright

Miss without one set off – We hated her and smoked her and baited her and I think drove her away. Miss B. thinks her a Paragon of fashion, and says she is the only woman she would change persons with. What a stupe – She is superior as a Rose to a Dandelion. When we went to bed Brown observed as he put out the taper what a very ugly old woman that Miss Robinson would make – at which I must have groaned aloud for I'm sure ten minutes.

... I never intend hereafter to spend any time with Ladies unless they are handsome – you lose time to no purpose.

What dreadful behaviour from the two men! We can only wonder that Fanny did not cut the relationship there and then; maybe it is a commentary on Georgian manners, for it was a brutal age.

Keats may not have had things all his own way, for a girl as attractive as Fanny Brawne would have enjoyed many admirers. She was a keen dancer, and the Long Room in Well Walk was close by. John didn't dance, and in February we find him asking his sister to teach him a few simple steps.

Because of the Brawnes' knowledge of their language, a number of Frenchmen visited the house. The French were refugees – men of status and education escaping the revolution in their own country. They came from a small colony at Oriel House, Hampstead, their numbers kept up by other victims of Napoleonic persecution. The Frenchmen had the charm of excellent good manners and etiquette far beyond those of Brown and Keats, and Keats viewed Miss Brawne's popularity with jealous eyes. Charles Dilke wrote, 'He don't like anyone to look at or speak to her.'

Keats' friends, seeing the effect that she was having upon him, began to dislike her, and they unkindly labelled her 'a vulgar suburban flirt'.

There is no doubt that the early stages of disease were beginning to affect Keats' mental state at this time. His sore throat returned time after time, and the mercury that he had taken in an effort to reduce the symptoms of some other mysterious complaint had left him in a highly nervous condition. From the Isle of Wight, where he had gone on a holiday with his friend James Rice, to escape from Wentworth Place and the close proximity of Fanny in order to work on his poetry, he wrote:

> I am in complete cue – in the fever ... My mind is heaped to the full; stuffed like a cricket ball ...

Just how he explained that he felt unable to write whilst near her we can't imagine! This state of mind made him grow resentful and irritable, and he wrote strange accusing letters to Fanny. As Haydon said, he did not 'bear the little sweet arts of love with patience'.

From the Isle of Wight in July he sent her one of the strange letters, and she replied archly that she must not have any more such letters. She tormented him further by telling of late-night parties and dancing. The following letter to Fanny was postmarked from Newport, 3 July 1819.

Shanklin, Isle of Wight.

My dearest Lady,
    I am glad I had not an opportunity of sending off a Letter which I wrote for you on Tuesday night – twas too much like one out of Rousseau's Heloise. I am more reasonable this morning. The morning is the only proper time for me to write to a beautiful Girl whom I love so much: for at night, when the lonely day has closed, and the lonely, silent, unmusical Chamber is waiting to receive me as into a Sepulchre, then believe me my passion gets entirely the sway, then I would not have you see those Rhapsodies which I thought it impossible I should ever give way to, and which I have often laughed at in another, for fear you should think me either too unhappy or perhaps a little mad. I am now at a very pleasant Cottage window, looking onto a beautiful hilly country, with a glimpse of the sea; the morning is very fine. I do not know how elastic my spirit might be, what pleasure I might have in living here and breathing and wandering as free as a stag about this beautiful Coast if the remembrance of you did not

weigh so upon me. I have never known any unalloyed Happiness for many days together: the death or sickness of some one has always spoilt my hours. [Death had stalked Keats since his childhood, but here he is thinking of his brother Tom.] And now when none such troubles oppress me, it is you must confess very hard that another sort of pain should haunt me. Ask yourself my love whether you are not very cruel to have so entrammelled me, so destroyed my freedom. . . .

For myself I know not how to express my devotion to so fair a form: I want a brighter word than bright, a fairer word than fair. I almost wish we were butterflies and lived but three summer days – three such days with you I could fill with more delight than fifty common years could ever contain. but however selfish I may feel, I'm sure I could never act selfishly: as I told you a day or two before I left Hampstead, I will never return to London if my Fate does not turn up Pam [a Pam is the knave of clubs in the game of Loo] or at least a Court-card. Though I could centre my Happiness in you, I cannot expect to engross your heart so entirely – indeed if I thought you felt as much for me as I do for you at this moment I do not think I could restrain myself from seeing you again tomorrow for the delight of one embrace. But no – I must live upon hope and Chance. In case of the worst that can happen, I shall still love you – but what hatred shall I have for another! Some lines I read the other day are continually ringing a peal in my ears: "To see those eyes I prize above mine own Dart favors on another – And those sweet lips (yielding immortal nectar) Be gently pressed by any but myself – Think, think Francesca, what a cursed thing It were beyond expression!" [from Philip Massinger's "Duke of Milan"] Do write immediately. There is no Post from this Place, so you must address Post Office, Newport, Isle of Wight. I know before night I shall curse myself for having sent you so cold a Letter; yet it is better to do it as much in my senses as possible. Be as kind as the distance will permit to your
  J. Keats

John wrote another letter on Thursday 8 July, in answer to one he had received from Fanny. Her letter has not survived, so there is no way to know when it was written. The post of the time must have been very fast if in fact she was writing in answer to his letter postmarked 3 July from the Isle of Wight.

8th July 1819

My sweet Girl,

Your Letter gave me more delight, than any thing in the world but yourself could do; indeed I am almost astonished that any absent one should have that luxurious power over my senses which I feel. Even when I am not thinking of you I receive your influence and a tenderer nature steeling upon me. All my thoughts, my unhappiest days and nights have I find not at all cured me of my love of Beauty, but made it so intense that I am miserable that you are not with me: or rather breathe in that dull sort of patience that cannot be called Life. I never knew before, what such a love as you have made me feel, was; I did not believe in it; my Fancy was affraid of it, lest it should burn me up. But if you will fully love me, though there may be some fire, 'twill not be more than we can bear when moistened and bedewed with Pleasures. . . . Why may I not speak of your Beauty, since without that I could never have loved you. I cannot conceive any beginning of such love as I have for you but Beauty. There may be a sort of love for which, without the least sneer at it, I have the highest respect and can admire it in others: but it has not the richness, the bloom, the full form, the enchantment of love after my own heart, so let me speak of your Beauty though to my own endangering; if you could be so cruel to me as to try elsewhere, its Power. You say you are affraid I shall think you do not love me – in saying this you make me ache the more to be near you. I am at the diligent use of my faculties here, I do not pass a day without sprawling some blank verse or tagging some rhymes, and here I must confess, that since I am on that subject, I love you the more in that I believe you have liked me for my own sake and for nothing else. I have met with women whom I really think would like to be married to a Poem and to be given away by a Novel. [Is Keats here thinking of Isabella Jones, whom he gave up in February?] I have seen your

Comet [on 26 June 1819 a comet passed across the face of the sun, but it was not visible before the early days of July], and only wish it was a sign that poor Rice would get well whose illness makes him rather a melancholy companion [James Rice, a friend of Keats, known to Fanny, had travelled to the Isle of Wight with Keats, and it seems he was always in poor health.]: and the more so as to conquer his feelings and hide them from me, with a forced Pun. I kissed your writing over in the hope you had indulged me by leaving a trace of honey. What was your dream? Tell it me and I will tell you the interpretation thereof.

 Ever yours, my love!
  John Keats

Do not accuse me of delay – we have not here an opportunity of sending letters every day. Write speedily.

Whilst Keats was on the Isle of Wight the two lovers probably corresponded on a weekly basis. From what Keats wrote to Fanny, we can assume that she kept her feet firmly on the ground at this time, and chided him for being too flowery in his language.

 The original of the following letter to Fanny has been mislaid, but we judge this to have been written a week after the last letter, on 15 July.

         Shanklin, Thursday Evening.

My Love,

 I have been in so irritable a state of health these two or three last days, that I did not think I should be able to write this week. Not that I was ill, but so much so as only to be capable of an unhealthy teasing letter. Tonight I am greatly recovered only to feel the languor I have felt after you touched with ardency. You say you perhaps might have made me better: you would then have made me worse: now you could quite effect a cure: What fee my sweet Physician would I not give you to do so. Do not call it folly, when I tell you I took your letter last night to bed with me. In the morning I found your name on the sealing wax obliterated. I was startled at the bad omen till I recollected that it must have happened in my dreams, and they you know fall out by contraries. You must have found out by this time I am a little given to bode ill like the Raven; it is my misfortune not my fault; it has proceeded from the general tenor of the circumstances of my life, and rendered every event suspicious. However I will no more trouble either you or myself with sad Prophecies; though so far I am pleased at it as it has given me opportunity to love your disinterestedness towards me. I can be a raven no more; you and pleasure take possession of me at the same moment. I am affraid you have been unwell. If through me illness have touched you (but it must be with a very gentle hand) I must be selfish enough to feel a little glad at it. Will you forgive me this? I have been reading lately an oriental tale of very beautiful colour [John Payne's translation of the Arabian Nights]. It is a city of melancholy men, all made so by this circumstance. Through a series of adventures each one of them by turns reaches some gardens of Paradise where they meet with a most enchanting Lady; and just as they are going to embrace her, she bids them shut their eyes – they shut them – and on opening their eyes again find themselves descending to the earth in a magic basket. The remembrance of this Lady and their delights lost beyond all recovery render them melancholy ever after. How I applied this to you, my dear; how I palpitated at it; how the certainty that you were in the same world with myself, and though as beautiful, not so talismanic as that Lady; how I could not bear you should be so you must believe because I swear it by yourself. I cannot say when I shall get a volume ready. I have three or four stories half done, but as I cannot write for the mere sake of the press, I am obliged to let them progress or lie still as my fancy chooses. By Christmas perhaps they may appear [no such collection ever appeared; maybe it was intended, but it would be a year before Taylor and Hessey published Keats' new book of poetry, and by that time he was very unwell and had little interest in the book], but I am not yet sure they ever will. It will be no matter, for Poems are as common as newspapers and I do not see why it is a greater crime in me than in another to let the verses of an half fledged brain tumble into the reading rooms and drawing room windows. Rice has been better lately than usual: he is not

suffering from any neglect of his parents who have for some years been able to appreciate him better than they did in his first youth, and are now devoted to his comfort. Tomorrow I shall, if my health continues to improve during the night, take a look farther about the country, and spy at the parties about here who come hunting after the picturesque like beagles. It is astonishing how they raven down the scenery like children do sweetmeats. The wondrous Chine here is a very great Lion: I wish I had as many guineas as there have been spy glasses in it. I have been, I cannot tell why, in capital spirits this hour. What reason? When I have to take my candle and retire to a lonely room, without the thought as I fall asleep, of seeing you tomorrow morning? or the next day, or the next – it takes on the appearance of impossibility and eternity – I will say a month – I will say I will see you in a month at most, though no one but yourself should see me; if it be but for an hour. I should not like to be so near you as London without being continually with you: after having once more kissed you Sweet I would rather be here alone at my task than in the bustle and hateful literary chitchat. Meantime you must write to me – as I will every week – for your letters keep me alive. My sweet Girl I cannot speak my love for you. Good night! and
    Ever yours
    John Keats

Ten days later he wrote again from Shanklin:

Sunday 25 July 1819.
Sunday Night.

My sweet Girl,

    I hope you did not blame me much for not obeying your request of a Letter on Saturday: we have had four in our small room playing at cards night and morning leaving me no undisturbed opportunity to write. Now Rice and Martin [John Martin, the publisher] are gone I am at liberty. Brown to my sorrow confirms the account you give of your ill health. You cannot conceive how I ache to be with you: how I would die for one hour – for what is in the world? I say you cannot conceive;

it is impossible you should look with such eyes upon me as I have upon you: it cannot be. Forgive me if I wander a little this evening, for I have been all day employed in a very abstract Poem ['Lamia'] and I am in deep love with you – two things which must excuse me. I have, believe me, not been an age in letting you take possession of me; the very first week I knew you I wrote myself your vassal; but burnt the Letter as the very next time I saw you I thought you manifested some dislike to me. If you should ever feel for Man at the first sight what I did for you, I am lost. Yet I should not quarrel with you, but hate myself if such a thing were to happen – only I should burst if the thing were not as fine as a Man as you are as a Woman. Perhaps I am too vehement, then fancy me on my knees, especially when I mention a part of your Letter which hurt me; you say speaking of Mr Severn ' but you must be satisfied in knowing that I admired you much more than your friend'. My dear love, I cannot believe there ever was or ever could be any thing to admire in me especially as far as sight goes – I cannot be admired, I am not a thing to be admired. You are, I love you; all I can bring you is a swooning admiration of your Beauty. I hold that place among Men which snubnosed brunettes with meeting eyebrows do among women – they are trash to me – unless I should find one among them with a fire in her heart like the one that burns in mine. You absorb me in spite of myself – you alone: for I look not forward with any pleasure to what is called being settled in the world; I tremble at domestic cares – yet for you I would meet them, though if it would leave you the happier I would rather die than do so. I have two luxuries to brood over in my walks, your Loveliness and the hour of my death. O that I could have possession of them both in the same minute [the 'Bright Star' sonnet]. I hate the world: it batters too much the wings of my self-will, and would I could take a sweet poison from your lips to send me out of it. From no others would I take it. I am indeed astonished to find myself so careless of all charms but yours – remembering as I do the time when even a bit of ribbon was a matter of interest with me. What softer words can I find for you after this – what it is I will not read. Nor will I say more here, but in a Postscript answer any thing else you may have mentioned in your Letter in so many words – for I am distracted with a thousand thoughts. I will imagine you Venus tonight and pray, pray, pray to your star like a Heathen.

    Yours ever, fair Star,
      John Keats

My seal is marked like a family table cloth with my Mother's initial F for Fanny: put between my Father's initials. You will soon hear from me again. My respectful Compts to your Mother. Tell Margaret I'll send her a reef of best rocks and tell Sam I will give him my light bay hunter if he will tie the Bishop hand and foot and pack him in a hamper and send him down for me bathe him for his health with a Necklace of good snubby stones about his Neck.

Margaret and Sam are Fanny's sister and brother; the Bishop is likely to have been a cat – it seems Keats wanted to drown the poor creature! This could have been the letter that Fanny objected to.

    The next letter he wrote over two days, Thursday the 5th and Friday, 6 August. It is postmarked Newport, 9 August 1819.

                                Shanklin Thursday Night.

My dear Girl,
    You say you must not have any more such Letters as the last: I'll try that you shall not by running obstinate the other way – Indeed I have not fair play – I am not idle enough for proper downright love-letters – I leave this minute a scene in our Tragedy and see you (think it not blasphemy) through the mist of Plots speeches, counter plots and counter speeches – The Lover is madder than I am – I am nothing to him [Ludolph in 'Otho the Great'] – he has a figure like the Statue of Maleager [in the Vatican] and double distilled fore in his heart. Thank God for my diligence! were it not for that I should be miserable. I encourage it, and strive not to think of you – but when I have succeeded in doing so all day and as far as midnight, you return as soon as this artificial excitement goes off more severely from the fever I am left in – Upon my soul I cannot say what you could like me for. I do not think myself a fright any more than I do Mr A Mr B. and Mr C.

yet if I were a woman I should not like A.B.C. But enough of this – So you intend to hold me to my promise of seeing you in a short time. I shall keep it with as much sorrow as gladness: for I am not one of the Paladins of old who lived upon water grass and smiles for years together – What though would I not give tonight for the gratification of my eyes alone? This day week we shall move to Winchester; for I feel the want of a Library. [Keats believed that he could find a good library in Winchester; however, he was to be disappointed.] Brown will leave me there to pay a visit to Mr Snook at Bedhampton: in his absence I will flit to you and back. I will stay a very little while, for I am in a train of writing now I fear to disturb it, let it have its course bad or good – in it I shall try my own strength and the public pulse. At Winchester I shall get your Letters more readily; and it being a cathedral City I shall have a pleasure always a great one to me when near a Cathedral, of reading them during the service up and down the Aisle. Friday Morning, just as I had written thus far last night, Brown came down in his morning coat and night-cap, saying he had been refreshed by a good sleep and was very hungry – I left him eating and went to bed being too tired to enter into any discussions. You would delight very greatly in the walks about here, the Cliffs, woods, hills, sands, rocks &c about here. They are however not so fine but I shall give them a hearty good bye to exchange them for my Cathedral – Yet again I am not so tired of Scenery as to hate Switzerland – We might spend a pleasant year at Berne or Zurich – if it should please Venus to hear my 'Beseech thee to hear us O Goddess" And if she should hear God forbid we should what people call settle – turn into a pond, a stagnant Lethe – a vile crescent, row or buildings. Better be imprudent movables than prudent fixtures. Open my Mouth at the Street door like the Lion's head at Venice to receive hateful cards Letters messages. Go out and wither at tea parties; freeze at dinners; bake at dances, simmer at routs. No my love, trust yourself to me and I will find you nobler amusements, fortune favouring. I fear you will not receive this till Sunday or Monday; as the Irishman would write do not in the mean while hate me – I long to be off for Winchester for I begin to dislike the very door posts here the names, the pebbles. You ask after my health, not telling me whether you are better. I am quite well. You going out is no proof that you are: how is it? Late hours will do you great harm. What fairing is it? I was alone for a couple of days while Brown went gadding over the country with his ancient knapsack. Now I like his society as well as any Man's, yet regretted his return – It broke in upon me like a Thunderbolt – I had got in a dream among my Books – really luxuriating in a solitude and silence you alone should have disturbed –

    Your ever affectionate
    John Keats

John did not return to London; he went straight from the Isle of Wight to Winchester, breaking his promise to Fanny.

Keats now seemed likely to stay away from London for the whole of the summer. He made no effort to make the promised visit to Fanny at Hampstead. Any engagement between them at this time was just a matter of an understanding; and if he felt free to do as he pleased, she could do likewise without an argument. That very summer there came a chance for Fanny to enjoy fashionable pursuits with her circle of friends. The Royal Artillery Mess at Woolwich held some of the best balls in London that year, and the Royal Artillery band played for them. Mrs Brawne had some contacts amongst the military, and Fanny went to the dances. She probably mentioned this in one of her letters, for Keats asks, 'What fairing is it?' He went out of his way to show his disapproval. 'I am no officer in yawning quarters,' he wrote, and the letter takes the tone which he himself called 'flint-worded'.

He did not write to Fanny from Winchester until two weeks after his arrival. When he did write, on 16 August, it was, in his mad hero Ludolph's words, to 'put on a judge's brow, and use a tongue made iron-stern by habit'!

Fanny had been offended that he had not made his promised visit, but she told him that he might do as he pleased!

He replied coldly that he could not do as he pleased, 'for my life is ruled by lack of money'.

Winchester. Monday 16 Aug 1819.

My dear Girl,

What shall I say for myself? I have been here four days and not yet written you – its true I have had many teasing letters of business to dismiss – and have been in the Claws, like a Serpent in an Eagle's, of the last act of our Tragedy [Act V of 'Otho the Great']. This is no excuse; I know it; I do not presume to offer it. I have no right either to ask a speedy answer to let me know how lenient you are – I must remain some days in a Mist – I see you through a Mist: as I dare say you do me by this time. Believe in the first Letters I wrote you: I assure you I felt as I wrote – I could not write so know. The thousand images I have had pass through my brain – my uneasy spirits – my unguess'd fate, all spread as a veil between me and you – Remember I have no idle leisure to brood over you – its well perhaps I have not. I could not have endured the throng of Jealousies ['The Cap and Bells'] that used to haunt me before I had plunged so deeply into imaginary interests. I would feign, as my sails are set, sail on without an interruption for a Brace of Months longer – I am in complete cue – in the fever; and shall in these four Months do an immense deal – This page as my eye skims over it I see is excessively unloverlike and ungallant – I cannot help it – I am no officer in yawning quarters; no Parson-Romeo. My mind is heaped to the full; stuffed like a cricket ball – if I strive to fill it more it would burst. I know the generality of women would hate me for this; that I should have so unsoftened so hard a Mind as to forget them; forget the brightest realities for the dull imaginations of my own Brain. But I conjure you to give it a fair thinking; and ask yourself whether 'tis not better to explain my feelings to you, than write an artificial Passion – Besides you would see through it. It would be vain to strive to deceive you. 'Tis harsh, harsh, I know it – My heart seems now made of iron – I could not write a proper answer to an invitation to Idalia [an invitation from Venus in Idalium, Cyprus, where she was worshipped]. You are my Judge: my forehead is on the ground. You seem offended at a little simple innocent childish playfulness in my last. I did not seriously mean to say that you were endeavouring to make me keep my promise. I beg your pardon for it. 'Tis but just your Pride should take alarm – seriously. You say I may do as I please – I do not think with any conscience I can; my cash resources are for the present stopped; I fear for some time. I spend no money but it increases my debts. I have all my life thought very little of these matters – they seem not to belong to me. It may be a proud sentence; but, by heaven, I am entirely above all matters of interest as the Sun is above the Earth – and though of my own money I should be careless; of my Friends I must be spare. You see how I go on – like so many strokes of a Hammer. I cannot help it – I am impelled, driven to it. I am not happy enough for silken Phrases, and silver sentences. I can no more use soothing words to you than if I were at this moment engaged in a charge of Cavalry – Then you will say I should not write at all – Should I not? This Winchester is a fine place: a beautiful Cathedral and many other ancient buildings in the Environs. The little coffin of a room at Shanklin is changed for a large room, where I can promenade at my pleasure – looks out onto a beautiful – blank side of a house. It is strange I should like it better than the view of the sea from our window at Shanklin. I began to hate the very posts there – the voice of the old Lady over the way was getting a great Plague. The Fisherman's face never altered any more than our black teapot – the nob however was knocked off to my little relief. I am getting a great dislike of the picturesque; and can only relish it over again by seeing you enjoy it. One of the pleasantest things I have seen lately was at Cowes. The Regent in his Yatch [this spelling of yacht was accepted at the time] (I think they spell it) was anchored opposite – a beautiful vessel – and all the Yatch's and boats on the coast, were passing and repassing it; and circuiting and tacking about it in every direction – I never beheld any thing so, silent, light and graceful – As we passed over to Southampton, there was nearly an accident. There came by a Boat well manned; with two naval officers at the stern. Our Bowlines took the top of their little mast and snapped it off close by the board – had the mast been a little stouter they would have been upset. In so trifling an event I could not help admiring our Seamen – Neither officer nor man in the whole Boat moved a Muscle – they scarcely noticed it even with words – Forgive me for this flint-worded Letter, and believe and see that I cannot think of you without some sort of energy – though mal a propos – Even as I leave off it seems to me that a few more moments' thought of you would uncrystallize and dissolve me. I must not give way to it – but turn to my writing again – if I fail I shall die hard.

O my love, your lips are growing sweet again to my fancy – I must forget them. Ever your affectionate
   Keats

Sometime early in September, a letter from his brother George in America came into Keats' hand. The news it contained was most disturbing: George was in serious financial difficulty. A business venture of his had failed. The letter begged John to intercede with Richard Abbey for the release of money owed to him from the estate of their brother Tom.

John set off for London, determined to confront Abbey with his brother's letter. He stopped first at the home of the Wylies – the family of his sister-in-law – where he began to disclose the contents of George's letter but thought better of it. He read it over to Mrs Wylie, skating over the worst of the news.

The meeting with Abbey went better than he could have hoped. He offered John a place in a hat-making business, and as they sat drinking tea in Abbey's office John waited for an opportunity to bring up the subject of money. Abbey produced a copy of the *St James Chronicle*, which he had probably saved for the occasion of a Keats visit, for it contained the first two cantos of Byron's new poem 'Don Juan' and a review of the work. Abbey was no lover of Byron, or any poet of the day, and he said the poem was the most licentious thing he had ever seen in the English press. However, he remarked, "The fellow says true things now and then." To Keats' annoyance he began reading, his voice full of sarcasm:

> What is the end of Fame? 'tis but to fill
> A certain portion of uncertain paper:
> Some liken it to climbing up a hill,
> Whose summit, like all hills, is lost in vapour:
> For this men write, speak, preach, and heroes kill,
> And bards burn what they call their 'midnight taper',
> To have, when the original is dust,
> A name, a wretched picture, and worse bust.

John held his temper, and he eventually got an advance of £200 (£100 for George and £100 for himself) together with a promise that his guardian would intercede with his Aunt Jennings over the matter of her proposed Chancery suit against the Keats family. (His aunt was suing for a greater share of her late father-in-law's estate – money that had been left to the Keats orphans.)

After leaving Abbey, Keats walked up Cheapside, and then turned towards Lombard Street and the general post office. He carried in his pocket a letter to Fanny that he had meant to post the day before, but he kept it there until he had missed the last post.

John had planned to spend three days in Town, but he stayed a day extra. What he did in this time remains a mystery. Twice he turned toward Hampstead, then turned away. He went to see his sister in Walthamstow; the Abbeys were unusually friendly, and he stayed for some time and left with his spirits raised.

A chance meeting with Richard Woodhouse lifted him further. Woodhouse supported Keats and admired his poetry. He was a lawyer, and a reader for the publishers Taylor and Hessey. John counted him a friend. The meeting gave them a chance to indulge in their shared liking for claret. They spent several hours at Woodhouse's rooms at The Temple, drinking and talking. Keats took the opportunity to show the red-headed lawyer some of his new poems.

Woodhouse then left for a holiday in Weymouth, and Keats walked with him to the coach office to see him off. As he watched the coach disappear in a cloud of dust, a feeling of deep loneliness came over him.

That same night, he boarded the coach for his return to Winchester. The letter to Fanny was burning a hole in his jacket pocket, and it pricked his conscience. Before he left, it was finally posted. Keats had been in London from the night of the 10th – four days had passed – and yet, for reasons that he could not fathom himself, he had avoided Hampstead and Fanny Brawne.

My dear Girl,

I have been hurried to Town by a Letter from my brother George; it is not of the brightest intelligence. Am I mad or not? I came by the Friday night coach and have not yet been to Hampstead. Upon my soul it is not my fault. I cannot resolve to mix any pleasure with my days: they go on one like another undistinguishable. If I were to see you today it would destroy the half comfortable sullenness I enjoy at present into downright perplexities. I love you too much to venture to Hampstead, I feel it is not paying a visit, but venturing into a fire. Que ferai-je? as the French novel writers say in fun, and I in earnest: really what can I do? Knowing well that my life must be passed in fatigue and trouble, I have been endeavouring to wean myself from you: for to myself alone what can be much of a misery? As far as they regard myself I can despise all events: but I cannot cease to love you. This morning I scarcely know what I am doing. I am going to Walthamstow. I shall return to Winchester tomorrow [the letter was dated the 13th, so why did he stay in town an extra day and travel back to Winchester on Wednesday, 15 September?], whence you shall hear from me in a few days. I am a Coward, I cannot bear the pain of being happy: 'tis out of the question: I must admit no thought of it.

    Yours ever affectionately
    John Keats

What effect a letter such as this must have had on the feelings of a young girl in love, we can only wonder at!

    The next letter Keats wrote to Fanny was not from Winchester, and it was written almost a month later than his last. He wrote from College Street, in Westminster, London, where he had taken up a lodging found for him by Dilke, for he still planned to live away from Hampstead and Fanny. He wanted to find a job writing for any publication that would employ him. He was prepared to do that which he had before said he would never do: write for money. However, he was irresistibly drawn to Wentworth Place and Fanny, and, in spite of what had passed between them, she received him warmly. The upshot of his meeting with her was that all his carefully made plans were up in the air. He decided to return to Brown and his old lodging in Wentworth Place, next door to Fanny.

How long Keats lived in the rooms at College Street is not known; however, it can only have been a matter of days rather than weeks. On Monday the 11th and Wednesday 13 October he wrote to Fanny from College Street, but by the 19th of the same month he wrote to her from Great Smith Street, where he was staying with Charles and Maria Dilke.

> Monday the 11th of October 1819.
> College Street.
>
> My sweet Girl,
> I am living to day in yesterday: I was in a complete fascination all day. I feel myself at your mercy. Write me ever so few lines and tell me you will never for ever be less kind to me than yesterday – You dazzled me. There is nothing in the world so bright and delicate. When Brown came out with that seemingly true story against me last night, I felt it would be death to me if you had ever believed it – though against any one else I could muster up my obstinacy. Before I knew Brown could disprove it I was for the moment miserable. When shall we pass a day alone? I have had a thousand kisses, for which with my whole soul I thank love – but if you would deny me the thousand and first – 'twould put me to the proof how great a misery I could live through. If you should ever carry your threat yesterday into execution – believe me 'tis not my pride, my vanity or any petty passion would torment me – really 'twould hurt my heart – I could not bear it. I have seen Mrs Dilke this morning; she says she will come with me any fine day.
> Ever yours
> John Keats

Ah hertè mine!

What could Fanny Brawne's threat have been that so stirred the poet? Maybe she told him that she had had enough of his strange behaviour, threatening to end the relationship if he did not mend his ways.

On 19 September Keats had written the ode 'To Autumn'. In his heart he knew that to give his mind over to Fanny, as he was about to do, would end his creativity; and, as history records, he wrote very little of merit beyond the winter of 1819.

On Wednesday 13 October 1819 he wrote to Fanny from his lodging at 25 College Street:

> My dearest Girl,
>
> This moment I have set myself to copy some verses out fair. I cannot proceed with any degree of content. I must write you a line or two and see if that will assist in dismissing you from my Mind for ever so short a time. Upon my Soul I can think of nothing else. The time is passed when I had power to advise and warn you against the unpromising morning of my Life. My Love has made me selfish. I cannot exist without you. I am forgetful of every thing but seeing you again – my Life seems to stop there – I see no further. You have absorbed me. I have a sensation at the present moment as though I was dissolving – I should be exquisitely miserable without the hope of soon seeing you. I should be affraid to separate myself far from you. My sweet Fanny, will your heart never change? My love, will it? I have no limit now to my love – Your note came in just here – I cannot be happier away from you. 'Tis richer than an Argosy of Pearls. Do not threat me even in jest. I have been astonished that Men could die Martyrs for religion - I have shuddered at it. I shudder no more – I could be martyred for my Religion – Love is my religion – I could die for that. I could die for you. My Creed is Love and you are its only tenet. You have ravished me away by a Power I cannot resist; and yet I could resist till I saw you; and even since I have seen you I have endeavoured often 'to reason against the reasons of my Love' [Ford's ''Tis Pity She's a Whore']. I can do that no more – the pain would be too great. My love is selfish. I cannot breathe without you.
>
> Yours for ever
> John Keats

Keats was finally suffering from the full force of an unfulfilled love infatuation. He was wound up, going far beyond what could be considered reasonable in his letters. In two poems that he wrote at the time his state of mind is illustrated to full effect.

Lines to Fanny

1

What can I do to drive away
Remembrance from my eyes? for they have seen,
Aye, an hour ago, my brilliant Queen!
Touch has a memory. O say, love, say,
What can I do to kill it and be free
In my old liberty?
When every fair one that I saw was fair
Enough to catch me in but half a snare,
Not keep me there:
When, howe'er poor or particoloured things,
My muse had wings,
And ever ready was to take her course
Whither I bent her force,
Unintellectual, yet divine to me; –
Divine, I say! – What sea-bird o'er the sea
Is a philosopher the while he goes
Winging along where the great water throes?

2

How shall I do
To get anew
Those moulted feathers, and so mount once more
Above, above
The reach of fluttering Love,
And make him cower lowly while I soar?
Shall I gulp wine? No, that is vulgarism,
A heresy and schism,

Foisted into the canon-law of love; –
No, – wine is only sweet to happy men;
More dismal cares
Seize on me unawares, –

3

Where shall I learn to get my peace again?
To banish thoughts of that most hateful land,
Dungeoner of my friends, that wicked strand
Where they were wreck'd and live a wrecked life;
That monstrous region, whose dull rivers pour
Ever from their sordid urns unto the shore,
Unown'd of any weedy-haired gods;
Whose winds, all zephyrless, hold scourging rods,
Iced in the great lakes, to afflict mankind;
Whose rank-grown forests, frosted, black, and blind,
Would fright a Dryad; whose harsh herbag'd meads
Make lean and lank the starv'd ox while he feeds;
There flowers have no scent, birds no sweet song,
And great unerring Nature once seems wrong.

4

O, for some sunny spell
To dissipate the shadows of this hell!
Say they are gone, – with the new dawning light
Steps forth my lady bright!
O, let me once more rest
My soul upon that dazzling breast!
Let once again these aching arms be plac'd,
The tender gaolers of thy waist!
And let me feel that warm breath here and there
To spread a rapture in my very hair, –

> O, the sweetness of the pain!
> Give me those lips again!
> Enough! Enough! it is enough for me
> To dream of thee!

This poem must have done little to lift Fanny's uneasiness about her relationship with the wayward poet. He complains that she is wrecking his life; he is starving; he does not enjoy wine or the song of birds. Not until the last stanza does he make any attempt to ease the pain of the preceding three. In stanza one line fourteen he even tells her that she is 'unintellectual'. Of course she was not considered to be an intellectual, but there was little need to commit the matter to print! A month later he writes of her again in 'Ode to Fanny'. This work is a little kinder to her than 'Lines to Fanny', but even here he is not considering her feelings. The whole work has a selfishness running though it. Neither poem can be considered to be amongst his great works.

Ode to Fanny

1

> Physician Nature! Let my spirit blood!
> O ease my heart of verse and let me rest;
> Throw me upon thy Tripod, till the flood
> Of stifling numbers ebbs from my full breast.
> A theme! a theme! great Nature! give a theme;
> Let me begin my dream.
> I come – I see thee, as thou standest there,
> Beckon me not into the wintry air.

2

> Ah! dearest love, sweet home of all my fears,
> And hopes, and joys, and panting miseries, –

To-night, if I may guess, thy beauty wears
A smile of such delight, As brilliant and as bright,
As when ravished, aching, vassal eyes,
Lost in a soft amaze,
I gaze, I gaze!

3

Who now, with greedy looks, eats up my feast?
What stare outfaces now my silver moon!
Ah! keep that hand unravished at the least;
Let, let, the amorous burn –
But pr'ythee, do not turn
The current of your heart from me so soon.
O! save, in charity,
The quickest pulse for me.

4

Save it for me, sweet love! though music breathe
Voluptuous visions into the warm air;
Though swimming through the dance's dangerous wreath,
Be like an April day,
Smiling and cold and gay,
A temperate lily, temperate as fair;
Then, Heaven! there will be
A warmer June for me.

5

Why, this, you'll say, my Fanny! is not true:
Put your soft hand upon your snowy side,
Where the heart beats: confess – 'tis nothing new –
Must not a woman be
A feather on the sea,

Sway'd to and fro by every wind and tide?
Of as uncertain speed
As blow-ball from the mead?

6

I know it – and to know it is despair
To one who loves you as I love, sweet Fanny!
Whose heart goes fluttering for you everywhere,
Nor, when away you roam,
Dare keep its wretched home,
Love, love alone, has pains severe and many:
Then, loveliest! keep me free, From torturing jealousy.

7

Ah! if you prize my subdued soul above
The poor, the fading, brief, pride of an hour;
Let none profane my Holy See of love,
Or with a rude hand break
The sacramental cake:
Let none else touch the just new-budded flower;
If not – may my eyes close,
Love! on their lost repose.

Oh, how the green-eyed monster holds sway throughout this poem! Keats worries about her dancing and holding hands with another man in stanza four, and in stanza five he asks her to, with hand on heart, confess her love for him alone. In the same stanza he attacks women for being feckless and fickle. (Charles Dilke: 'He don't like no one to look at her'!)

Fanny copied the sonnet 'Bright Star' into her pocketbook, Keats had given her a copy of the work sometime towards the end of 1819. She must have believed that it was written for her. Joseph Severn found Keats with another version of the poem during the voyage to Italy, and he believed it to be the last spark of his friend's genius. However, the first version was written, we believe, early in 1819. It may have even been for Isabella Jones, as the poem was in a softer vein than the two later works, 'Lines to Fanny' and 'Ode to Fanny'. Perhaps Keats gave Fanny the 'Bright Star' sonnet to salve his conscience.

In September and October his reading and study had been from the works of Burton. By the middle of October he was nearing the end of Burton's third treatise on love-melancholy, studying the prognostics of love-melancholy and the cure of love-melancholy. In the margins, at the end of the lines that he approved of, he wrote, 'Aye' or 'Good'. Unfortunately he began to apply Burton's methods to his own situation.

'All Lascivious meats must be forsaken' was the recommendation to overcome physical passion; Keats spoke to Brown about a vegetarian diet. This diet, he told Fanny, he must impose upon himself now that he had come to live next door to her again.

In 'Ode to Fanny', the first line ('Physician Nature! Let my spirit blood!') refers to the letting of blood, which was recommended at the time for ailments of the body and mind. The line is straight from Burton. On the next page, Keats read, 'Blood-letting above the rest will make lovers come to themselves, and keep in their right mind.'

Keats describes his own physical condition: 'My temples with hot jealous pulses beat.' His jealousy was as violent as any on the pages of Burton's work. His mind was in a frenzied state, just a month after the period of calm at Winchester. He wrote, 'I cry your mercy – pity – love! – aye, love!' Maybe disease, the tuberculosis bacillus, was even then growing within him. If so, this may account for his warped sense of judgement, for the contrast with the recent months of calm at Winchester, where he had completed some of his most beautiful works, is striking and rapid. From his mother's side of the family he had inherited his strong passionate nature; this nature, the foundation of his genius, now threatened to destroy him.

In a new period of calmness he wrote the sonnet:

The Day Is Gone

The day is gone, and all its sweets are gone!
Sweet voice, sweet lips, soft hand, and softer breast,
Warm breath, light whisper, tender semitone,
Bright eyes, accomplis'd shape, and lang'rous waist!
Faded the flower and all its budded charms,
Faded the sight of beauty from my eyes,
Faded the shape of beauty from my arms,
Faded the voice, warmth, whiteness, paradise!
Vanish'd unseasonably at shut of eve,
When the dusk holiday – or holinight –
Of fragrant-curtain'd love begins to weave
The woof of darkness thick, for hid delight:
But, as I've read love's missal through to-day,
He'll let me sleep, seeing I fast and pray.

It's difficult to deduce the true character of Frances Brawne. There is no doubt that during the first year of her acquaintance with Keats she was a little flighty, but by the time of his death she had acquired a certain maturity.

Joseph Severn was much taken by her mother, who seems to have been a kind and gentle woman, in spite of the fact that she termed Keats "that mad boy"! However, Severn had little time for her daughter, and could not understand his friend's attraction to her. Her own attraction to Keats was plain for him to see, but it was a long time before he realised how fatal the attraction had been. The Reynolds family hated her, calling her "that poor idle thing of womankind to whom he has so unaccountably attached himself". The Dilkes agreed that the attachment was a misfortune for Keats, although they bore Fanny no ill will. As for Brown, he must have known her better than anyone. He was a long-standing friend of the Brawne family. He invited Fanny up to his rooms, where he flirted unmercifully with her, as Keats, lying ill downstairs, squirmed in his secret agony.

A cousin of the Brawne family, who visited Wentworth Place as a young boy about 1819/20, gave his impressions of Fanny in an article published in the *New York Herald* on 12 April 1889, but his impressions are likely to have been distorted over time:

> Miss Fanny Brawne was very fond of admiration. I do not think she cared for Keats, although she was engaged to him. She was very much affected when he died, because she had treated him so badly. She was very fond of dancing, and of going to the opera and to balls and parties. Miss Brawne's mother had an extensive acquaintance with gentlemen, and the society in which they mingled was musical and literary. Through the Dilke's Miss Brawne was invited out a great deal, and as Keats was not well enough to take her out himself (for he never went with her), she used to go with military men to the Woolwich balls and to balls in Hampstead; she danced with these military officers a great deal more than Keats liked. She did not seem to care much for him. Mr Dilke, the grandfather of the present Sir Charles Dilke, admired her very much in society, and although she was not a great beauty she was very lively and agreeable. I remember that among those frequenting Mrs Brawne's house in Hampstead were a number of foreign gentlemen. Keats could not talk French as they could, and their conversation with his fiancee in a language he could not understand was a source of continual disagreement between them. Keats thought that she talked and flirted and danced too much with them, but his remonstrance's were all unheeded by Miss Brawne.

Against this should be set Fanny's own writings in later years, which seem to show a true, and even tender, understanding of the poet's character, if not his genius. On Tuesday 19 October Keats wrote from Great Smith Street, Westminster, where he had gone to stay with the Dilkes. He had just spent three days at Hampstead, close to Fanny, and he had made up his mind to venture again into the fire.

My sweet Fanny,

On awakening from my three days dream ('I Cry to Dream Again') [Shakespeare's *The Tempest*] I find one and another astonished at my idleness and thoughtlessness. I was miserable last night – the morning is always restorative. I must be busy, or try to be so. I have several things to speak to you of tomorrow morning. Mrs Dilke I should think will tell you that I purpose living at Hampstead. I must impose chains upon myself. I shall be able to do nothing. I should like to cast the die for Love or death. I have no Patience with any thing else – if you intend to be cruel to me as you say in jest now but perhaps may sometimes be in earnest be so now – and I will – my mind is in a tremble, I cannot tell what I am writing.

Ever my love yours
John Keats

After John had been back in Hampstead for a short time, Charles Brown noted a change in the poet: he had given up serious work and was in a highly nervous and agitated state.

In January, the severe winter of 1819/20 continued unabated. Keats' sore throat had returned, and the weather was against him going out. He moped around the house, watching the comings and goings of the Brawnes from the parlour window. Brown tried without success to lift John's melancholy, and then by chance Abigail O'Donaghue, Brown's servant girl, found a bottle of laudanum by his chair. Keats admitted using the drug and Brown made him promise to stop at once, but it's unlikely he kept his promise.

Towards the end of January the weather improved; the long cold spell broke, and February set in warmer. Keats paid a long-delayed visit to town. On the night of Thursday the 3rd he returned to Hampstead, riding on the outside of the coach without his greatcoat. He stumbled into Wentworth Place, hardly able to stand.

Brown could see at once that he was seriously ill, and he directed him straight to bed. Keats was trembling violently, and as he slipped between the cold sheets he coughed and blood came into his mouth.

"This blood is my death warrant," he said as a shocked Brown looked on.

The next morning, lying exhausted in his bedroom, covered with blankets, he managed to write a short note to Fanny. He dated the note 4 February 1820, and Brown sent it round to the Brawnes by his servant Abigail.

> Dearest Fanny,
> I shall send this the moment you return. They say I must remain confined to this room for some time. The consciousness that you love me will make a pleasant prison of the house next to yours. You must come and see me frequently: this evening, without fail – when you must not mind about my speaking in a low tone for I am ordered to do so though I can speak out.
> Yours ever
> sweetest love
> J. Keats
>
> turn over [he continued overleaf]
>
> Perhaps your Mother is not at home and so you must wait till she comes. You must see me tonight and let me hear you promise to come tomorrow. Brown told me you were all out. I have been looking for the stage the whole afternoon. Had I known this I could not have remained so silent all day.

When Fanny came to the sickbed we don't know, but when she finally arrived she sat by him in a stunned silence as he tried, speaking in a low voice, to reassure her about his health. It was obvious from his pale complexion that he had suffered a severe setback. Everyone at that time was well aware of tuberculosis – a disease few survived. It's likely that Fanny was at home on the morning after John's first haemorrhage, and that to keep him quiet Brown told him that she was out. The lie was meant kindly, but it had the opposite effect. Keats had been looking for her all the previous afternoon, from time to time raising himself from the bed to look out of the window in the hope of seeing the town coach coming up the hill towards the Bird in Hand in the High Street. Movement would not have helped his damaged lungs.

At last he began to suspect that he was being fobbed off. Why had Fanny not been to see him? He questioned Brown, who said that maybe her mother was out, and that she was waiting for her to return.

After this there were regular visits from Fanny. The two began an exchange of little notes, and every evening she sent round a goodnight message.

Somewhere about this time Keats must have written his last few poetic lines – eight lines, which were obviously meant for Fanny:

This Living Hand

> This living hand, now warm and capable
> Of earnest grasping, would, if it were cold
> And in the icy silence of the tomb,
> So haunt thy days and chill thy dreaming nights
> That thou wouldst wish thine own heart dry of blood
> So in my veins red life might stream again,
> And thou be conscience-calm'd – see here it is –
> I hold it towards you.

We do not know if she ever saw this; but if she did, she would have realised that he had a conviction that his death was inevitable.

A week passed since the first haemorrhage; then, on 10 February, he wrote a longer letter and sent it round to next door by Brown's servant.

Thursday the 10th of February. (By Hand)

My Dearest Girl,
    If illness makes such an agreeable variety in the manner of your eyes I should wish you sometimes to be ill. I wish I had read

your note before you went last night that I might have assured you how far I was from suspecting any coldness. [Keats is referring to her silence.] You had a just right to be a little silent to one who speaks so plainly to you. You must believe – you shall, you will – that I can do nothing, say nothing, think nothing of you but what has its spring in the Love which has so long been my pleasure and torment. On the night I was taken ill – when so violent a rush of blood came to my Lungs that I felt nearly suffocated, I assure you I felt it possible I might not survive, and at that moment thought of nothing but you. When I said to Brown 'this is unfortunate' I thought of you. 'Tis true that since the first two or three days other subjects have entered my head. I shall be looking forward to Health and the Spring and a regular routine of our old walks.

Your affectionate
J.K.

The notes from Keats to Fanny Brawne during the time of his illness number at least twenty-nine. The last directly to her is written in the August. His very last letter to the family is to Mrs Brawne, Fanny's mother. He wrote it whilst the *Maria Crowther* was held in quarantine in Naples Harbour. Although not addressed to Fanny, I'm sure his intention was that she would see it.

How many notes Fanny sent to John during that first stage of his illness is not known. None have survived.

By 9 February John had been moved from his bedroom at the rear of the house to a comfortable bed in the front parlour. He describes the move in a letter to his sister:

> How much more comfortable than a dull room up stairs, where one gets tired of the pattern of the bed curtains. Besides I see all that passes – for instance now, this morning – If I had been in my own room I should not have seen the coals brought in. On Sunday between the hours of twelve and one I descried a Pot boy. I conjectured it might be the one o'Clock beer.

At that time the area around Wentworth Place was open heathland. The view from the front of the house was clear except for two properties in the process of being built. One of these – Eton Lodge – stands today. The heath was common land used for grazing animals and by local washerwomen for drying clothes. There were always people moving about on the heath.

In a letter to his sister in Walthamstow, John describes what he saw from the window of the parlour:

> Old women with bobbins and red cloaks and unpresuming bonnets I see creeping about the heath. Gipsies after hare skins and silver spoons. Then goes by a fellow with a wooden clock under his arm that strikes a hundred and more. Then comes the old French emigrant (who has been very well to do in France) with his hands joined behind on his hips, and his face full of political schemes. . . . As for those fellows the Brickmakers they are always passing to and fro. I mus'n't forget the two old maiden Ladies in Well Walk who have a Lap dog between them that they are very anxious about. It is a corpulent Little beast whom it is necessary to coax along with an ivory-tipp'd cane. Carlo our Neighbour Mrs. Brawne's dog and it meet sometimes. Lappy thinks Carlo a devil of a fellow and so do his Mistresses. Well they may – he would sweep 'em all down at a run; all for the Joke of it.

Keats was now on a diet to the point of starvation. This, with the constant bleeding performed by Dr Sawrey, had weakened him beyond measure. Brown called in another doctor, Dr Rodd, who lived nearby and was able to call on the patient daily. Rodd and Brown discussed bringing in a specialist for another opinion. Dr Robert Bree, an Oxford MD and a leading expert of the day on respiratory disease, was brought in. Bree had written a thesis on asthma that became the reference book of the time. He took Keats off the starvation diet, and stopped the blood-letting.

Early in March, Keats suffered another attack, coughing up blood from his lungs. He also had a panic attack and violent palpitations. Dr Bree held out hope of recovery, saying that he found no pulmonary infection and no organic defects. He advised no reading or poetry-writing, or anything that might excite or stress his patient. Fanny Brawne's visits were limited so as not to disturb the calming process. Dr Bree, a man of seventy, had yet to see the stethoscope. It was invented in Paris only the previous year. If he had used such a piece of equipment, he would have detected the bacillus in his patient's lungs.

Keats wrote to his sister, Fanny, on 20 March 1820:

> My Dear Fanny –
> According to your desire, I write to-day. It must be but a few lines, for I have been attack'd several times with a palpitation at the heart and the Doctor says I must not make the slightest exertion. I am much the same to-day as I have been for a week past. They say 'tis nothing but debility and will entirely cease on my recovery of my strength which is the object of my present diet. As the Doctor will not suffer me to write I shall ask Mr. Brown to let you hear news of me for the future if I should not get stronger soon. I hope I shall be well enough to come and see your flowers in bloom.
> Ever your most affectionate Brother
> John

Fanny Brawne's visits were reduced; he had to be satisfied with her daily notes and occasional glimpses of her through the window. He wrote to her, 'Let me no longer detain you from going to town – there may be no end to this imprisoning of you.' He also suggested that he should free her from their engagement: 'I wish I had even a little hope'. Fanny refused to break off their engagement. She felt closer to him now that he was ill; since the beginning of his illness she had felt a new tenderness toward him. Before, she had taken their love for granted; but now, with his brother Tom's recent death from the same disease, she began to realise that she might lose him. After her refusal to give him up, he wrote:

> My greatest torment since I have known you has been a fear of you being a little inclined to the Cressid; but that suspicion I dismiss utterly and remain happy in the surety of your Love, which I assure you is as much a wonder to me as a delight.

Fanny gave him a ring engraved with their names. The gift delighted him more than anything before, and he picked up his pen to write:

> The power of your benediction is of not so weak a nature as to pass from the ring in four and twenty hours – it is like a sacred Chalice once consecrated and ever consecrate. I shall kiss your name and mine where your Lips have been – Lips! why should a poor prisoner as I am talk about such things. Thank God, though I hold them the dearest pleasure in the universe, I have a consolation independent of them in the certainty of your affection. I could write a song in the style of Tom Moore's Pathetic about Memory if that would be any relief to me. No 'twould not. I will be as obdurate as a Robin. I will not sing in a cage.

About the middle of March, a new diet containing meat and fish had restored some of Keats' strength. On his better days he was able to go for short walks with Fanny about the heath, and on the 25th he was well enough to take up Haydon's invitation to attend the private viewing of the artist's giant painting of *Christ Entering Jerusalem*.

Brown must have noticed that Fanny now never visited the house when he was at home. Keats had asked her not to. Brown joked and flirted with Fanny, and she laughed louder than she should have done – a laugh made the more nervous by the pained, jealous look in John's eyes. He began to be suspicious and jealous of everything she did. Having begged her to take up her old lifestyle, he now began to question her about where she went and whom she had been with.

Both Fanny and Brown must have had their patience sorely tried, for it's unlikely that Keats could always contain his irritability and hostile moods.

A small happening at the beginning of April broke the monotony of the invalid's life. His sister's guardian, Richard Abbey, took a dislike to her pet spaniel and threatened to turn it loose. For the sake of his sister, and the poor animal, John agreed to take the dog in at Hampstead.

Fanny must have cared for it for a time, although Keats' reservations about revealing his feelings for her seem to have precluded his mentioning this to his sister. It was not possible for Fanny Brawne to care for the spaniel for long, as Carlo, the Brawnes' large mongrel dog, became exceedingly jealous of the new arrival. John wrote to his sister, 'The Dog is being attended to like a Prince.'

Where the little dog finally found a home is unclear. Maria Dilke is said to have sent it to her brother-in-law, her husband's brother William, who lived close by, but it may have gone to the Snooks at Bedhampton. This is the most likely explanation. John Snook was in fact Charles Dilke's brother-in-law.

In April Keats had to face being parted from his love. Brown was making plans for another Scottish tour, and, as he planned to rent out his part of Wentworth Place for the summer, it was necessary for Keats to move out. Biographers have accused Brown of selfishness, but he had supported Keats to some extent financially, as well as spending the last two months nursing his friend. He needed the funds from the rental for his own holiday expenses.

Leigh Hunt had recently moved to an address in Kentish Town – 13 Mortimer Terrace – and he arranged lodgings for Keats at 2 Wesleyan Place, a house very near to his own.

Keats moved into the accommodation there on 4 May. Charles Brown paid the cost of the move and a week's rent in advance. He did not ask for the six weeks' rent owed him by John, or the cost of his food and wine for that period, the bill for which had been greater than usual as he had followed Bree's recommendation to build up his patient's strength. There is no doubt that Brown felt responsible for his friend. He borrowed £50 from his lawyer, and this he gave to him towards his living expenses.

A few days after moving, John wrote to Fanny from his new address:

> My dearest Girl,
> I endeavour to make myself as patient as possible. Hunt amuses me very kindly – besides I have your ring on my finger and your flowers on the table. I shall not expect to see you yet because it would be so much pain to part with you again. When the Books you want come you shall have them. I am very well this afternoon.

Keats spent a quiet week marking the pages in his Spenser, finding passages that he believed she would like. Although with his medical knowledge it is unlikely that he was ever deceived about his condition, on 15 May he wrote to Brown, saying he 'felt well enough to extract more pleasure than pain from the summer'. This feeling of well-being was not to last. By the end of May he wrote to Fanny the first of his most disturbing letters, as bitterness and jealousy began to overcome his judgement:

> My dearest Girl,
> I wrote a letter for you yesterday, expecting to have seen your mother. I shall be selfish enough to send it though I know it may give you a little pain, because I wish you to see how unhappy I am for love of you, and endeavour as much as I can to entice you to give up Your whole heart to me whose whole existence hangs upon you. you could not step or move an eyelid but would shoot to my heart – I am greedy of you. Do not think of anything but me. Do not live as if I was not existing – Do not forget me – But have I any right to say you forget me? Perhaps you think of me all day. Have I any right to wish you to be unhappy for me? You would forgive me for wishing it, if you knew the extreme passion I have that you should love me – and for you to love me as I do you, you must think of no one but me, much less write that sentence. Yesterday and this morning I have been haunted with a sweet vision – I have seen you the whole time in your shepherdess dress. How my senses have ached at it! How my heart has been devoted to it! How my eyes have been full of Tears at it! Indeed I

think a real Love is enough to occupy the widest heart – Your going to Town alone, when I heard of it was a shock to me – yet I expected it – promise me you will not for some time, till I get better. Promise me this and fill the paper full of the most endearing names. If you cannot do so with good will, do my Love tell me – say what you think – confess if your heart is too much fasten'd on the world. Perhaps then I may see you at a greater distance, I may not be able to appropriate you so closely to myself. Were you to loose a favourite bird from the cage, how would your eyes ache after it as long as it was in sight; when out of sight you would recover a little. Perhaps if you would, if so it is, confess to me how many things are necessary to you besides me, I might be happier, by being less tantaliz'd. Well may you exclaim, how selfish, how cruel, not to let me enjoy my youth! to wish me to be unhappy! You must be so if you love me – upon my Soul I can be contented with nothing else. If you could really what is call'd enjoy yourself at a Party – if you can smile in peoples faces, and wish them to admire you now, you never have nor ever will love me. I see life in nothing but the certainty of your Love – convince me of it my sweetest. If I am not somehow convinc'd I shall die of agony. If we love we must not live as other men and women do – I cannot brook the 'wolfsbane' of fashion and foppery and tattle. You must be mine to die upon the rack if I want you. I do not pretend to say I have more feeling than my fellows – but I wish you seriously to look over my letters kind and unkind and consider whether the Person who wrote them can be able to endure much longer the agonies and uncertainties which you are so peculiarly made to create – My recovery of bodily health will be of no benefit to me if you are not all mine when I am well. For God's sake save me – or tell me my passion is of too awful a nature for you. Again God bless you

    J.K.

No – my sweet Fanny – I am wrong. I do not want you to be unhappy – and yet I do, I must while there is so sweet a Beauty – my loveliest my darling! Good bye! I Kiss you – O the torments!

Other letters in similar vein followed. Keats accused Fanny of flirting with Brown and tried to stop her visits to the Dilkes. He wrote:

> When you are in the habit of flirting with Brown you would have left off, could your own heart have felt one half of one pang mine did. Brown is a good sort of Man – he did not know he was doing me to death by inches. . . . though I know his love and friendship for me, though at this moment I should be without pence were it not for his assistance, I will never speak to him until we are both old men, if we are to be.

John's mind was filled with suspicion and bitterness, and his irrational behaviour was directed at those who were his friends. At the Dilkes' house he began an argument and behaved badly. Afterwards he wrote:

> I forsee I shall know very few people in the course of a year or two. . . . I am weary of the world.

An added worry was his sister's difficult relationship with her guardian, Richard Abbey. She sent him a letter requesting help, but as he went to catch the Walthamstow coach for a meeting with the Abbeys his mouth filled with blood. He was forced to return to Wesleyan Place.

His landlady called on the Hunts with news of her lodger's distress. Keats was now a patient of a Dr Lambe, who had been recommended by Leigh Hunt. Lambe said that he could not be left alone in his lodging, and the Hunts decided to move him into their own home at Mortimer Terrace. Hunt was himself suffering from a fever at the time, and his wife had been a consumptive for some months. The Hunts lived their lives in continuous muddle and harassment; they were always short of money and struggled to meet day-to-day expenses. The house was cramped; there were too many children, for the Hunts' family grew at an alarming rate! Charles Brown remarked, "Will Hunt ever stop?" However, the kindly Hunts would always find room for a friend in need.

At the end of June the weather became very warm, but Keats was in no fit state to take advantage of it. He endured his stuffy imprisonment, sweating, often with blood coming into his mouth. Another doctor was called in.

He and Dr Lambe agreed that their patient would not survive another English winter, and that his only chance lay in travelling to Italy. From then on plans were made for Keats to journey abroad.

To take advantage of the weather, and to get him out of the house for a time, Hunt took him for a drive in the coach up to Hampstead. They sat together on a bench in Well Walk, near to the Bentleys' house, where Tom had suffered so greatly during his last hours. Keats began to reminisce about his brother, and at last he broke down. Hunt said, "He turned to me, his eyes full of tears, and told me that his heart was broken."

Sometime about 10 August a letter came from Fanny, redirected from his lodging to the Hunts'. Their young maid took it in at the door. Mrs Hunt may have been busy about the house; in any case, she asked the girl to give it to John, but she put it in her apron pocket and there it stayed. She may have simply fogotten about it, but it seems that she objected to the extra work the presence of the sick poet was making for her, and she had already decided to look for new employment.

Two days after its delivery, the letter was handed to Keats by Hunt's young son Thornton. John saw that the seal had been broken. It appears that the letter contained little of any consequence, but because it was from Fanny he became utterly distraught. What would have been a small incident for him two years before, now pushed him over the edge. He broke down and wept. Hunt tried to calm him, offering his humble apologies, but Keats was beyond consolation. He left the house, stumbling along blindly; he decided to see Fanny and explain that he could no longer stay with the Hunts, but he hesitated to call at Wentworth Place. Instead he decided to go further on to Well Walk, to the house of Bentley, the postman. Mrs Bentley had been more than a landlady to the Keats boys; she had become their friend.

Whilst in Kentish Town, and before the delayed-letter affair, Keats had written what would be his last letter to Fanny Brawne. The letter has no date or postmark and was probably delivered by hand. He must have written it late at night for he says, 'I do not write this till the last that no eye may catch it.'

My dearest Girl,

I wish you could invent some means to make me at all happy without you. Every hour I am more and more concentrated in you; every thing else tastes like chaff in my Mouth. I feel it almost impossible to go to Italy – the fact is I cannot leave you, and shall never taste one minute's content until it pleases chance to let me live with you for good. But I will not go on at this rate. A person in health as you are can have no conception of the horrors that nerves and temper like mine go through. What island do your friends propose retiring to? I should be happy to go with you there alone, but in company I should object to it; the backbitings and jealousies of new colonists who have nothing else to amuse themselves, is unbearable. Mr Dilke came to see me yesterday, and gave me a very deal more pain than pleasure. I shall never be able any more to endure the society of any of those who used to meet at Elm Cottage and Wentworth Place. The last two years taste like brass upon my Palate.

['Hyperion', Book 1 lines 188–9: 'his ample palate took | Savour of poisonous brass and metal sick'.] If I cannot live with you I will live alone. I do not think my health will improve much while I am separated from you. For all this I am averse to seeing you, I cannot bear flashes of light and return into my glooms again. I am not so unhappy now as I should be if I had seen you yesterday. To be happy with you seems such an impossibility! it requires a luckier Star than mine! it will never be. I enclose a passage from one of your letters which I want you to alter a little – I want (if you will have it so) the matter express'd less coldly to me. If my health would bear it, I could write a Poem which I have in my head, which would be a consolation for people in such a situation as mine. I would show some one in Love as I am, with a person living in such Liberty as you do. Shakespeare always sums up matters in the most sovereign manner. Hamlet's heart was full of such Misery as mine is when he said to Ophelia "Go to a Nunnery, go, go!" Indeed I should like to give up the matter at once – I should like to die. I am sickened at the brute world which you are smiling with. I hate men and women more. I see nothing but thorns for the future – wherever I may be next winter in Italy or nowhere Brown will be living near you with his indecencies – I see no prospect of any rest. Suppose me in Rome – well, I should there see you as in a magic glass going to and from town at all hours. – I wish you could infuse a little confidence in human nature into my heart. I cannot muster any – the world is too brutal for me – I am glad there is such a thing as the grave – I am sure I shall never have any rest till I get there. At any rate I will indulge myself by never seeing any more Dilke or Brown or any of their Friends. I wish I was either in your arms full of faith or that a Thunder bolt would strike me.

God bless you.

J.K.

The 'God bless you' may be the only saviour of this terrible letter. Note that he has taken to signing off his letters to Fanny with just J.K. or J. Keats; one might have thought that he would have used John at the very least. This is another sign of his brutish manner at this time. This mood of destruction cannot be laid at the door of tuberculosis alone. It is likely that Keats was still using laudanum, the opium-based medication of the time, to ease the pain in his chest. We do not know how Fanny replied to these letters, but we know she forgave him completely, as this is borne out by her manner later.

Keats never made it to Well Walk – his legs failed him. When he arrived at Wentworth Place he stood in the doorway, where Mrs Brawne found him, a picture of utter dejection. Seeing the state he was in, she generously suggested that he should stay, and she and Fanny cared for him during the time left to him in England.

Keats' life's work was done. His new book of poems had been published in the first week of July. It contained 'Lamia',

'Isabella' (or 'The Pot of Basil'), 'The Eve of St Agnes', and other poems. Taylor, Keats' publisher, said that if the book didn't sell well, 'I think nothing will ever sell well again', but by this time the poet had no interest one way or another.

September dawned with cold winds in the evenings. The time had come for Keats to go if he would go at all. As yet it had not been settled who would travel with him. Brown was in Scotland and there had been no reply to the letter that Keats had sent informing him of his plans. Fanny wanted to go – if they would be married, she would travel as his wife. Mrs Brawne reluctantly agreed, and she said she would go also.

Although he must have been tempted, John felt he must refuse. He could not put Fanny through the drawn-out agony of attending his deathbed. The memory of Tom's suffering during his last days was still fresh in his mind. From Fanny's mother, too, it would be expecting too much.

To cheer each other, Fanny and Keats talked of his return the next summer.

As time drew near for his departure, the question as to who would accompany him to Italy was still unresolved. On 13 September William Haslam, who had offered himself as the organiser for Keats' journey, called on Joseph Severn – 'our oak friend' as Severn had named him. Straight away Haslam gave the reason for the visit: would Severn be prepared to go with Keats? Severn had seen little of Keats during the summer; his painting commissions gave him little time for leisure. He had thought that John's health was improving under the care of Fanny and her mother; he did not know that the journey to Italy was almost settled. Without it seems a moment's hesitation Severn answered, "I'll go."

Keats was packed up and ready. The last painful goodbyes were said. He asked Fanny to write to his sister on his behalf, telling her of his departure and exhorting her to be careful of the Abbeys and to look after her health. This first letter between the two Fannys paved the way for a long-lasting friendship.

John and Fanny exchanged locks of hair. He gave her his miniature by Severn. Each wore the other's ring. She stitched a silk lining into his travelling cap, and gave him a pocket diary and a penknife. They walked together to the coach station, and, as the coach was about to depart, with tears in her eyes she slipped a last personal gift into his hand. It was a large white cornelian in the shape of an egg. This was an intimate and personal gift, for it was something that she had used to cool her hands whilst at her needlework. During his final days of suffering it was never to leave his hands.

On Wednesday, 13 September, Fanny wrote in her copy of *The Literary Pocket-Book*, which had been published by Leigh Hunt the year before, 'Mr Keats left Hampstead.' (As the book was for 1819, she made the entry against 8 September, the second Wednesday for that year.)

Frances Brawne wrote the following letter to Keats' sister, including lines dedicated by John, dated 11 September, in which he said, 'It is not illness that prevents me writing, but as I am recommended to avoid every sort of fatigue, I have accepted the assistance of a friend who I have desired to write to you when I am gone, and communicate any intelligence she may hear of me'. These lines are in Fanny Brawne's hand and signed by her. Keats never wrote another letter to his sister or to Fanny Brawne.

                        Monday afternoon. September 18, 1820.

My dear Miss Keats,
   Your brother on leaving England expressed a wish that I should occasionally write to you; a wish with which I feel the greatest pleasure in complying, but I cannot help thinking I require some kind of introduction, instead of which I must inform you of all my claims to your correspondence and I assure you I think them no slight ones, for I have known your brother for two years, am a great friend of Mrs Dilke's who I believe you like, and once sent you a message, which I do not know whether you received by a lady who had then never seen you but who expected to do so, a

Mrs Cornish. Besides which I have several times invited you to stay with me during the last time your brother George was in England, an indulgence which was not granted me. You see I have been quite intimate with you, most likely without you ever having heard my name. Besides all this your brother has been staying with us for the last six weeks of his being in this country and my mother nursed him. He left us last Wednesday but as the ship waited a few days longer than we expected, he did not sail from London till 7 o'clock yesterday morning. This afternoon we have received letters from two of his friends [likely to have been John Taylor and William Haslam] who accompanied him as far as Gravesend; they both declare his health and spirits to be better than they could have expected. I do not enclose you the letters or send you all the particulars because Mr Haslam said he should call on you very soon and he may have seen you before you receive this note; if that should not be the case, you will be pleased to hear that he went part of the way with him: his kindness cannot be described. As he was uneasy at your brother's travelling by himself he persuaded a friend [Joseph Severn] to go with him, and in a few weeks Mr Brown, who you probably Know by name will follow him. [Brown did not travel to Italy until after Keats' death. He arrived there in August 1822.] I cannot tell you how much every one have exerted themselves for him, nor how much he is liked, which is the more wonderful as he is the last person to exert himself to gain people's friendship. [She goes on to write those famous lines that can be found in so many works about the poet.] I am certain he has some spell that attaches them to him, or else he has fortunately met with a set of friends that I did not believe could be found in the world. May I hope, at some time to receive a letter from you? Perhaps you have an objection to write to a stranger. If so, I will try not to be very much disappointed if your objection is too strong to be overcome. For my own part I have long ceased to consider you a stranger and though this first letter may be a little stiff – because I wish to let you know what a time I have been acquainted with you, it will not be the case again, for at any rate I shall write once more whether you answer or not, as soon as letters are received from your brother, which I hope will not be for some time, for writing agitates him extremely. In Mr

Haslam you will see the best person in the world to raise your spirits, he feels so certain your brother will soon recover his health. What an unconscionable first letter. I remain yours, allow me to say, affectionately.

Frances Brawne

Although Fanny Keats did correspond many times with Frances Brawne, none of her letters survive, for Miss Brawne must not have taken care to save them. However, Keats had sometime before asked his sister to keep all letters safely, thinking that in posterity they would have some value. This request Fanny Keats complied with to the letter, and in so doing she garnered so much that would have been lost for ever otherwise.

Fanny Brawne's first letter definitely fixes the date that Keats left Hampstead as Wednesday 13 September. In the intervening days, before he boarded the *Maria Crowther* on the 17th at Tower Dock, he was with his publisher, John Taylor, at Fleet Street, where certain documents were drawn up and signed.

It seems that Fanny Keats readily agreed to correspond with her namesake, for on 6 October Fanny Brawne sent another letter to Walthamstow:

Friday night. October 6. 1820.

My Dear Miss Keats,

First I must return you my thanks for your readiness in accepting me as a correspondent, and then hasten to inform you I have heard of your brother. I received yesterday a letter from Mrs Dilke with part of a letter from a relation of hers [Mr John Snook, her husband's brother-in-law, the miller from Bedhampton], copied out for my benefit, as I shall copy it for yours. "John Snook writes" I have had some very un-expected visitors, Mr Keats and Mr Severn. They had been beating about with a contrary wind ever since they left London, and at last put into Portsmouth. I think Mr Keats much better than I expected and Mr Severn said he was sure that notwithstanding the hardships they had undergone, he was much better than when he left London.'

I cannot say this news pleases me much, I was in hopes that by this time he was half-way to Naples. He left Portsmouth on the 29th of September, the wind being favorable, the next day it changed again contrary to their wishes, but they did not return so it is supposed the captain put to Sea. I had a message for you from your brother before he left Hampstead as well as a lock of hair, both of which I forgot. He particularly requests you will avoid colds and coughs, and desires you never to go into the cold air out of the hothouse. The hair I myself cut off for you. It is very short as he had little at the time. If you wish to use it in a manner that requires more pray mention it, I have some that was cut off two or three years ago I believe, and there is no difference in color. [It was the practice of the time to make gifts of hair to lovers and close friends. The hair would be fashioned into rings, or fixed in a decorative manner on to card.] The Mrs Cornish I mean visits a family of the name of Goss or something like it; she told me she was frequently in the habit of calling, with them, on Mr and Mrs Abbey; but if she described her intimacy falsely, all I can say is that she is a foolish woman and if ever I see her again, I will ask her what she could mean. At any rate, her daughter, whose name is Grace, remembers you about six years ago, but she was so stupid I could make her understand nothing. My Mother is just returned from the city, and she saw Mr Haslam who had received a letter from Mr Severn [Severn's letter describes their ordeal on board the *Maria Crowther*, beating down the Channel], not dated so late by some days as that Mrs Dilke received; Mr Keats had had no return of his complaint, and had suffered comparatively little sea-sickness. I believe we shall receive that letter or one like it shortly. If that is the case I will send it to you or copy it for you. I will not make any request about a speedy answer but leave it to your own inclinations.

Your affectionate Friend
Frances Brawne

In her next letter to Fanny Keats, Francis Brawne wrote, 'We have received a letter from your brother.' She refers to a letter that Keats had written from Naples Harbour whilst held in quarantine there. The letter is addressed to her mother, for Keats never wrote directly to Fanny after he left England. However, he would have known that she would see it.

Tuesday 24th Oct: 1820.

My dear Mrs Brawn –

A few words will tell you what sort of a Passage we had, and what situation we are in, and few they must be on account of the Quarantine, our Letters being liable to be opened for the purpose of fumigation at the Health Office. [The *Maria Crowther* was being held in quarantine because of a suspected outbreak of cholera in London. The letter, which survives today, is very discoloured, possibly by the fumigation.] We have to remain in the vessel ten days and are at present shut in a tier of ships. The sea air has been beneficial to me about to as great an extent as squally weather and bad accommodations and provisions has done harm. So I am about as I was. Give my Love to Fanny and tell her, if I were well there is enough in this Port of Naples to fill a quire of Paper – but it looks like a dream – every man who can row his boat and walk and talk seems a different being from myself. I do not feel in the world. It has been unfortunate for me that one of the Passengers is a young Lady in a Consumption – her imprudence has vexed me very much – the knowledge of her complaints – the flushings in her face, all her bad symptoms have preyed upon me – they would have done so had I been in good health. Severn now is a very good fellow but his nerves are too strong to be hurt by other people's illnesses – I remember poor Rice wore me in the same way in the Isle of Wight – I shall feel a load off me when the Lady vanishes out of my sight. It is impossible to describe exactly in what state of health I am – at this moment I am suffering from indigestion very much, which makes such stuff of this Letter. I would always wish you to think me a little worse than I really am; not being of a sanguine disposition I am likely to succeed. If I do not recover your regret will be softened – if I do your pleasure will be doubled. I dare not fix my Mind upon Fanny, I have not dared to think of her. The only comfort I have had that way has been in thinking for hours together of having the knife she gave me put in a silver-case – the hair in a Locket – and the Pocket Book in a gold net. Show her this. I dare say no more. Yet you must not believe I am so ill as this Letter may look, for if ever there was a person born without the faculty of hoping I am he. Severn is writing to Haslam, and I have just asked him to request Haslam to send you his account of my health. O what an account I could give you of the Bay of Naples if I could once more feel myself a Citizen of this world – I feel a spirit in my Brain would lay it forth pleasantly – O what a misery it is to have an intellect in splints! My love again to Fanny – tell Tootts I wish I could pitch her a basket of grapes [Tootts was a pet name for Margaret, Fanny's sister] – and tell Sam the fellows catch here with a line a little fish much like an anchovy, pull them up fast. Remember me to Mr. and Mrs. Dilke – mention to Brown that I wrote him a letter at Portsmouth which I did not send and am in doubt if he ever will see it.

My dear Mrs. Brawne, yours sincerely and affectionate
John Keats

On 27 November 1820 Frances Brawne wrote again to Fanny Keats:

Monday Morning November 27, 1820.

My dear Friend,

I do not know whether you will consider mine a long silence but I can assure you it has not been the effect of forgetfulness. I was staying in town at the time your letter arrived, and though I soon returned home it was only for a few days. Besides which I thought it would be better to wait a short time in consequence of what you mentioned about Mrs Abbey. I was not quite a stranger to your situation in that family and I should write a eulogium on that lady's character in particular but I am affraid of some unlucky accident which might expose at the same time my opinion and our correspondence. Even now I tremble at what I have said as I am ignorant whether you receive your letters in public or whether you have private arrangements for that purpose. We received a letter from your brother about a fortnight ago. So I dare say did you. I was so extremely happy to hear of his arrival at Naples, that I overlooked the hardships of their wretched voyage and even the bad spirits he wrote in. The weather was so much against him, joined to his spirits which prey on him and continually make him worse, that it would have been too much to expect any great improvement in his health. He mentioned that Mr Severn was writing to Mr Haslam and that we should have the letter to read, as it would give a better account of him than he could write himself. However we have not yet received it. When it arrives I will copy any material part for you. I promised to do so before, when I received a former letter of Mr Severn's which arrived while I was in London. It was dated a day or two before their stay at Portsmouth and said your brother was a little better and that his spirits were good, which I think most material.

I saw that unlucky Mrs Cornish a short time before I received your last letter. By way of saying something I began to talk about you. Of course I did not tell her she had been suspected as an impostor, but I talked as carelessly as if our acquaintance had been formed on Mrs Abbey's recommendation. When I read your letter I was sorry for what I had done, so if I see her again I mean to insist that her ears have deceived her and that I did not say I had heard from you but of you from your brother. Not that I expect her to remember a word about it, or even that either of us exists. She said she was soon going to stay with Mrs Goss and that she should most likely call with her on your family. I saw Mrs Dilke the other day and delivered your message. She desires me to return her love. My Mother with an elderly lady's decorum begs to be remembered to you (and I beg for the future that you will always take it for granted she does so, as I am apt to forget her messages) and I send you my most affectionate love.

The two young ladies, from being chance acquaintances in the September, have by the November become firm friends – a friendship that goes beyond their mutual interest in the fate of John Keats.

Fanny Brawne began her next letter in the afternoon of 5 December.

> My dear Girl,
> I am affraid you will think me a most troublesome correspondent but this time I do not write on my own account but by your brothers wish. Mr Brown has received a letter from him dated November the 2nd [In this letter Keats begs Brown to look after Fanny. He writes, 'for my sake be her advocate for ever'.] from which I find he has not yet written to you, as he wished someone to do it for him. [Keats sent no letter directly to his sister from Italy. We can only surmise her feelings on the matter.] In the letter we received before dated the 24th of October, he said they had to stay on board ten days longer to perform Quarantine. So far they had had a tolerable voyage from the time they left Portsmouth. He did not think himself better or worse but his spirits were not very good. When he wrote to Mr Brown they were just arrived on shore, their sufferings during the quarantine were beyond any thing we can imagine. From your brother I never expect a very good account, but you may imagine how lowering to the spirits it must have been when Mr Severn who I never imagined it was possible for any thing to make unhappy, who I never saw for ten minutes serious, says he was so overcome that he was obliged to relieve himself by shedding tears. [Joseph Severn wrote to Haslam on 1 November, 'For myself I have stood it firmly until this morning when in a moment my spirits dropped at the sight of his suffering.'] He however says your brother was a little recovered, at least quite as much so as he could expect, the day after his arrival. He says, if he can but get his spirits good, he will answer for his being well in a moderate time; which shows he does not consider he has any complaint of consequence. [The true state of Keats' health was for their sakes hidden from both Fanny Brawne and his sister at this time.] They had met with several friends who were extremely kind to them, particularly the brother of a young lady passenger with them, who went out in dreadful health [Charles Cotterell, brother of another consumptive aboard the *Maria Crowther*: the young Miss Cotterell.] and who, God knows,

I have a thousand times wished at the bottom of the sea as I know she made it worse for your brother. The Physician to whom our friends were recommended was at Rome when they reached Naples and they had made up their minds to go to Rome. [This was Dr James Clark, who attended Keats in Rome.] I have written to him today and directed the letter there. [Although the letter arrived in Rome, Keats did not open it; neither did he read any other of his letters from England. It is said that they were placed in his coffin and buried with him.] If you would like to write to him mention it, and I will get the direction, for I cannot give it you now as it is a foreign one and I should make some mistake so I will ask Mr Brown again when I see him. I should like to have given you a better account but I must say that considering all things it is as well as we could have expected. My dear you must not consider this a letter from me but from your brother, for I should be quite ashamed not to mention being frightened of an acquaintance of yours – a letter has been received from Mrs George Keats to her brother. They are all very well and you may by this time, expect another little nephew or niece. [The child was a girl named Rosalind. She would die young, predeceasing her father.]

    Yours very affectionately
        Frances B.

January 15, 1821.

My dear Miss Keats

I am almost ashamed to write to you though I have been waiting for above three weeks to do so, but I hope you will forgive me, for it is not quite my fault. On the 23rd of December, Mr Brown received a letter from your brother in which he desired that someone would write to you to say he is as well as he could expect, and that we should hear from him in a few days [This letter, sent from Rome on 30 November 1820, was probably the last from his own hand. In it Keats asks Brown to send a note to his sister who 'walks about my imagination like a ghost – she is so like Tom'.] This letter I waited for some time, but as we have received since that a letter from Mr Severn, in which no mention is made of it I conclude he changed his mind fearful that the exertion might fatigue him. When

Mr Severn wrote, they were in Rome after a most wretched journey. They lodged opposite an English Physician [Dr James Clark, later to be Sir James Clark] to whom they were recommended, and who paid them the greatest attention. Your brother went out on horseback every day. [In his letter to Brown, Keats said, 'yet I ride the little horse'.] I am extremely glad they have chosen Rome instead of Naples for their winter residence. I am sure the climate is far preferable beside the disturbed state Naples seems likely to be in, and which no doubt induced them to quit it. Do, My dear Girl, if you have any intelligence of them, let me know it, however trifling we shall feel it of greatest consequence. The time is so long before either party can receive letters, that it makes me very impatient. My Mother desires her best remembrances to you, and believe me to remain

Yours most affectionately
Frances Brawne

This letter must have been started on the Monday morning, for Frances Brawne wrote in pencil on the inside cover, 'Tuesday, Rabbits Tuesday, January 16th 1821.' We can only guess at the meaning of this. She did on occasion keep pet rabbits, but the note could refer to a special day in the calendar year.

February 1st Hampstead. 1821.

My dear Girl

I have been this week wishing to write to you but putting it off every day in hopes of having something concerning your brother to communicate which would not give you pain, but it is vain to wait any longer. Oh my dear, he is very ill, he has been so ever since the 8th of December. If I had written this letter two hours sooner I should have owned to you that I had scarcely a hope remaining and even now when I have just received a letter from Mr Severn with the nearest approaching to good news that we have had since his last attack, there is nothing to rest upon, merely a hope, a chance. But I will tell you all in as collected a way as I can. On the 10th of January Mr Brown received a letter from Rome saying your brother had been attacked with spitting of blood and that the symptoms were very bad. He had been ill for 17 days and did not appear to get better. I judged of you by myself, and though I was then about to write I deferred it for some time in hopes a letter more cheering might arrive. I cannot think I was wrong. If you knew how much I regretted that it had not been kept from me [For reasons of misplaced kindness, Brown and her mother had kept the worst of the news from Fanny. In a letter to Severn, Brown wrote, in the middle of January, 'Miss Brawne does not actually know there is no hope she looks more sad every day. She has insisted on writing to him by this post, take care of the letter – if too late, let it be returned unopened to Mrs Brawne.'] – How continually I thought a fortnight or even a weeks ignorance of it would have been more pain spared – and when at last I could not bear to keep silence any longer for fear you should fancy the least neglect should have occasioned it, I wrote a letter that without mentioning any thing positively bad, did not, if I may judge from your answer give any hopes of a speedy recovery. Once or twice we have heard slight accounts, which were neither calculated to raise or depress our hopes but yesterday I was told of a letter from the Physician which said he was exactly the same. [Dr Clark said, 'The state of his mind is the worst possible for one in his condition, and will undoubtedly hurry on an event that I fear is not far distant.'] He did not get better nor did he get worse. But could I conceal from myself that with him, not getting better was getting worse? if ever I gave up hope, I gave it up then. I tried to destroy it, I tried to persuade myself that I should never see him again.

I felt that you ought no longer to remain in ignorance and the whole of this day I have been thinking how I could tell you. I am glad, very glad, I waited, for I have just received the account I spoke of in the beginning of this letter. Mr Severn says that for the first time he feels a hope, he thinks he shall bring him back to us. [Severn wrote to Fanny's mother, 'I most certainly think that I shall bring him back to England,' but then he goes on to contradict his statement with 'He has now given up all thoughts, hopes, or even wish for recovery. His mind is in a state of peace for the final leave he has taken of this world and all its future hopes. He sends his compliments to Miss Brawne, O! I would my unfortunate friend had never left your Wentworth Place – for the hopeless advantages of this comfortless Italy. He has many, many times talked over "the few happy days at your house, the only time when his mind was at ease".'] Surely, that is saying a great deal – and yet the reason he gives for that hope destroys it. Mr Severn says, for the last 3 days your brother had been calm, he had resigned himself to die. Oh can you bear to think of it, he has given up even wishing to live – Good God! is it to be borne that he, formed for everything good, and, I think I dare say it, for every thing great, is to give up his hopes of life and happiness, so young too, and to be murdered, for that is the case, by the mere malignity of the world, joined to want of feeling in those who ought above all to have felt for him – I am sure nothing during his long illness has hurt me so much as to hear he was resigned to die. But I will say no more about it. In a week or ten days I will enclose you the letter. You should have it sooner but we are obliged, in consequence of a message respecting money to send it to a friend in London first. [This was John Taylor, Keats' publisher, who had advanced money to support Keats and Severn in Italy. There had been a misunderstanding by the Italian bankers, Toronia, as to how the funds should be advanced. Taylor took steps so that the drafts were honoured at presentation.] And now my dear Girl, my dear Sister for so I feel you to be, forgive me if I have not sufficiently softened this wretched news. Indeed I am not now able to contrive words that would appear less harsh – If I am to lose him I lose every thing and then you, after my Mother will be the only person I shall feel interest or attachment for – I feel that I love his sister as my own – God bless you, he has talked of you continually, he did so when he was in great danger last spring. [Fanny here is referring to that first severe haemorrhage and the beginning of consumption in February 1820.] He has also expressed a wish for my Mother and Mrs Dilke to call on you. I cannot give up a hope that you may one day come and see me. Do you think Mr Abby will ever be induced to give his consent. If you think so whenever you write, tell me, and my Mother should ask his permission, but not just at present unless you think that would not be venturing too far at first.

    I remain my dearest Girl
        Yours very affectionately
           Fanny

> I forgot to mention he reads no letters for fear of agitating himself – I know I may trust to you never to mention me either now – or at any future time as connected with your brother as I know he would dislike that sort of gossiping way in which people not concerned mention those things – God bless you once more.

The final few lines in this letter confirm just how strongly Frances Brawne regarded her engagement to Keats as a personal matter. Her reply to Brown's request to publish some of the Keats poems in his possession (a request he made to her by letter eight years after the poet's death) expresses the same strong conviction.

Fanny Brawne's next letter to Keats' sister Fanny was dated on Monday morning, 26 February 1821. She was unaware that Keats had died on the 23rd, three days before. The letter contained little of consequence, but Fanny enclosed the letter from Severn to her mother referred to in her previous correspondence.

Charles Brown, after hearing of Keats' death, wrote to Joseph Severn and mentions Fanny Brawne:

> It is now five days since she heard it. I shall not speak of the first shock, nor of the following days, it is enough she is now pretty well and thro' out she has shown a firmness of mind which I little expected from one so young, and under such a load of grief.

It was to be 27 March before Fanny was able to put pen to paper and express her grief to the sister of Keats:

> Tuesday Afternoon March 27, 1821.
>
> You will forgive me, I am sure, my dear Fanny, that I did not write to you before, I could not for my own sake and I would not for yours, as it was better you should be prepared for what, even knowing as much as you did, you could not expect. I should like to hear that you my dearest Sister are well, for myself, I am patient resigned, very resigned. I know my Keats is happy,

happier a thousand times than he could have been here, for Fanny, you do not, you never can know how much he has suffered. So much that I do believe, were it in my power I would not bring him back. All that grieves me now is that I was not with him, and so near it as I was. Some day my dear girl I will tell you the reason and give you additional cause to hate those who should have been his friends, and yet it was a great deal through his kindness for me for he foresaw what would happen, he at least was never deceived about his complaint, though the Doctors were ignorant and unfeeling enough to send him to that wretched country to die, for it is now known that his recovery was impossible before he left us, and he might have died here with so many friends to soothe him and me, me with him. All we have to console ourselves with is the great joy he felt that all his misfortunes were at an end. At the very last he said 'I am dying thank God the time is come', and in a letter from Mr Severn written about a fortnight before he died and which was not shown to me, so that I thought he would live months at least, if he did not recover, he says 'he is still alive and calm, if I say more it will be too much, yet at times I have thought him better but he would not hear of it, the thought of recovery is beyond every thing dreadful to him – we dare not perceive any improvement for the hope of death seems his only comfort, he talks of the quiet grave as the first rest he can ever have. In that letter he mentions that he had given directions how he would be buried, the purse you sent him and your last letter (which he never read, for he would never open either your letters or mine after he left England) with some hair, I believe mine, he desired to be placed in his coffin. The truth is I cannot very well go on at present with this, another time I will tell you more, what I wish to say now relates to yourself, my Mother is coming to see you soon. If you are in Pancrass lane she will call next Friday, that is if it be not disagreeable to Mr Abby. [Brown wrote to Severn on 23 March: 'I wrote to Haslam to call on Abbey, and if Abby will permit it, Mrs Brawne and Mrs Dilke will call on Miss Keats. They are in mourning next door.'] Do you think he would allow you to stay with us a short time? I have desired my Mother to ask him, though I do not know how she will prevail on herself to do it, for she is affraid of him, but Mrs Dilke will be with her to give her courage. And now my dear I must hope you will favor me with your company, it will I assure you be a real favor. And yet I hardly like to press you to make such a dull visit. I once hoped for a very different one from you, I used to anticipate the pleasure I should feel in showing every kindness and attention in my power to you. And I felt so happy when he desired me to write to you while he was away. I little thought how it would turn out. I have just recollected that perhaps you will not wish to come out so soon. Fix your own time my dear, only come. Will you have the kindness to write to me, by return of post, if you can, to say if Friday will be too soon for you to see my Mother, and if you will come, and when. I ask you with more confidence though there is little or nothing to amuse with us, because I have heard you lead a very dull life in Mr Abbys family –but we will do as much as we can to amuse you and to prevent your thinking of any thing to make you unhappy. You must consider my Mother as more than a stranger for your brother loved her very much, and used often to wish she could go with him, and had he returned I should have been his wife and he would have lived with us. [Here Fanny Brawne confirms her engagement to Keats and her plans as his future wife.] All, all now in vain – could we have foreseen – but he did foresee and every one thought it was only his habit of looking for the worst. Though you are the only person in the world I wish to see, I will own I do not expect it. Your Guardian is said to be so much more than strict, and was so particular in refusing to let your brothers take you out, that I have not the least hope, but as much as we can do shall, with your consent, be tried and if it is in vain I will, before you leave London, call on you – If Mr Abby should so far think of it to ask who we are, you may if you like say my Mother is a widow and has two children besides me, both very young – send me an answer as soon as you can conveniently – My mother desires her love to you and I send a thousand good wishes to my dear sister God bless her.

Frances Brawne

People who knew Fanny Brawne at this time said that the loss of Keats had had a deep effect upon her. Her hair had lost its lustre and her thin face was deathly pale and wan. Brown said that she walked the heath alone, continually following the ways that she walked with Keats.

The next letter that we have was dated 23 May 1821. It is a long letter and has an importance, because in it she wrote of her feelings towards Keats. Although Frances Brawne wrote other letters to Keats' sister after this one, this is the last time she wrote about John.

Hampstead May 23, 1821.

My dear Fanny,

I find by my pocket book it is above 3 weeks since I received your letter and I am affraid you must have thought me neglectful in not writing before but as I have been staying that time in London and wished, when I did write to mention several things, I put it off till I should be by myself at home – In the first place only think of that Mrs Abbey after her promises to my Mother behaving as she has done. Not that I expected any thing better from her. Oh my dear, what a woman for a girl to be brought up with – The description I have had of her manners and conversation has quite shocked me. For you to look forward to 3 years more of it is dreadful – I find from my Mother that Mrs Dilke was foolish enough to mention me to her in a way I so much wished to avoid, but she appeared to know it already [the talk was of Fanny's engagement to Keats] and my Mother suspects from other things that passed, that she has read some of our letters. Do you think it possible, that she or any one of the family could get at them? You must know best, if you are sure it could not be the case I shall know my Mother was mistaken and that Mrs A. must have obtained her knowledge by some other means for you see she was better acquainted with Mrs Cornish than you supposed, indeed I should not have mentioned it at all but to put you on your guard. Should my opinion of her ever come to her ears she would prevent all intercourse between us, and really I could hardly blame her for so doing. . . . I thought when I began to write that I had a great deal to say and now I find I have half filled this letter without a word of what I had intended. I have not mentioned your brother. To no one but you would I mention him. I will suffer no one but you to speak to me of him. They are too uninterested in him to have any right to mention what is to you and me, so great a loss. I have copied a letter from Mr Severn giving an account of the last days of his life. No one knows I have it but you, and I had not sealed it up, as I thought you might wish to see it, but if you do, you must prepare for great pain, if you would rather not make yourself again unhappy, do not read it, I think you will be wise. It took me a long time to write. I have not looked at it since, nor do I mean to do so at present, but I mention it to you because though it gives pain, it also gives a certain kind of pleasure in letting us know how glad he was to die at the last. Dear Fanny, no one but you can feel with me – All his friends have forgotten him, they have got over the first shock, and that with them is all. They think I have done the same, which I do not wonder at, for I have taken care never to trouble them with any feelings of mine, but I can tell you who next to me (I must say next to me) loved him best, that I have not got over it and never shall – It's better for me that I should not forget him but not for you, you have other things to look forward to – and I would not have said any thing about him for I was affraid of distressing you but I did not like to write to you without telling you how I felt about him and leaving it to you whether the subject should be mentioned in our letters – In a letter you sent me some time ago you mentioned your brother George in a manner that made me think you had been mislead about him. He is no favorite of mine and he never liked me so that I am not likely to say too much in his favor from affection for him. but I must say I think he is more blamed than he should be. I think him extravagant and selfish but people in their great zeal make him out much worse than that – Soon after your brother Tom died, my dear John wrote to him offering him any assistance or money in his power. At that time he was not engaged to me and having just lost one brother felt all his affection turned towards the one that remained – George I dare say at first had no thoughts of accepting his offers but when his affairs did not succeed and he had a wife and one child to support, with the prospect of another, I cannot wonder that he should consider them first and as he could not get what he wanted without coming to England he unfortunately came – By that time your brother wished to marry himself, but he could not refuse the money. It may appear very bad in George to leave him 60 pounds when he owed 80, but he had many reasons to suppose the inconvenience would not last long. Your brother had a book of poems nearly ready to come out (which his illness kept back till the summer) he had a tragedy which Mr Brown calculated his share of would be about two hundred pounds and he was writing a story which had he lived to finish would if the others failed make up for it at least so every one imagined. [The book of poems contained 'Lamia', 'Isabella' (or 'The Pot of Basil'), 'The Eve of St Agnes', and other poems. The tragedy was 'Otho the Great', and the story that she refers to must have been 'The Cap and Bells'.] – George could not forsee his illness – He might be a cause of the dreadful consequences but surely a very indirect and accidental one. At the same time I cannot defend him, lately his behaviour has been very selfish and I may say shuffling. As to his returning the money I don't believe he has ever had it in his power to return a farthing or will ever have, that may not be his fault. The person who suffered most never thought so very badly of it, he used to say, George ought not to have done this he should have recollected that I wish to marry myself – but I suppose having a family to provide for makes a man selfish – They tell me that latterly he thought worse of George, but I own I do not believe it – One thing is against him. I don't think he could ever have supposed it would be in his power to return the money, at best not for many years – his brother never expected it at all, he always said he would not succeed – if when I write again I think of any thing for or against him I shall mention it – For I wish at any rate to put you on your guard – I have said I think him selfish – and I am affraid whenever you have your money in your own power you will find him troublesome but my dear girl be very cautious, be warned by what has already happened and remember he is extravagant at least every one says so. I don't know whether you will be able to connect and read all this – write as soon as you can – ever your affectionate sister and friend.

    Fanny

In this letter we note that Fanny Brawne spells Abbey correctly; before this she had written *Abby*. Also, she dated this letter at the beginning as the 23rd, but as the postmark is the 21st she made an error of two days.

The letter that Fanny copied in part for Fanny Keats was from the original written to John Taylor by Joseph Severn, dated 16 April 1821. The excerpt is as follows:

> Four days previous to his death – the change was so great that I passed each moment in dread, not knowing what the next would have – He was calm and firm at its approaches to a most astonishing degree. He told me not to tremble for he did not think that he should be convulsed; he said "did you ever see any one die?" "no" "well I pity you, poor Severn. What trouble and danger you have got into for me – now you must be firm for it will not last long. I shall soon be laid in the quiet grave – O! I can feel the cold earth upon me – The daisies growing over me – O for this quiet – it will be my first" – When the morning light came and still found him alive how bitterly he grieved – I cannot bear his cries – Each day he would look up in the Doctor's face to discover how long he should live he would say "how long will this posthumous life of mine last" that look was more than we could ever bear. The extreme brightness of his eyes with his poor pallid face were not earthly. These four nights I watched him, each night expecting his death – on the 5th day the Doctor prepared me for it. At 4 o'clock in the afternoon the poor fellow bade me lift him up in bed, he breathed with great difficulty and seemed to lose the power of coughing up the phlegm, an immense sweat came over him so that my breath felt cold to him. "Don't breathe on me it comes like ice" he clasped my hand very fast as I held him in my arms. The phlegm rattled in his throat, it increased but still he seemed without pain, he looked upon me with extreme sensibility but without pain, at 11 he died in my arms.

This excerpt was marked on the outside 'Sheet 2. from Mr Severn April 16th.'

This is the letter that Taylor passed to Isabella Jones, and the one about which she was most scathing, saying to Taylor, "such sickening sentimentality".

The last letter we have that Fanny Brawne wrote to Keats' sister is dated 16 June 1824. On the day that she received it she became of age – that is, twenty-one. Fanny Keats was born on 3 June 1803.

As time moved on and the truth became mixed with myth and legend, and as Fanny Brawne's letters were either destroyed or suppressed, the slander and innuendo continued.

An article on supposed Keats heroines, published by Katherine Tynan, did nothing to improve the much maligned lady's image:

> Fanny Brawne was a commonplace girl and incorrigible flirt who's behaviour made the last years of the poets life the more miserable.

Then from obscurity there appeared Rose Perrins of Forest Hill. She was the daughter of George Ramsey Todd, who had been a surgeon living in Hampstead. Dr Todd had at one time attended Keats. The family it seems had been close friends of the Brawne family. Mrs Perrins put her pen to paper refuting the new accusations:

> It is not true! Miss Brawne was my mother's great friend, and I knew her well up to the time I was almost fifteen, when she left England. She was a very striking dignified woman; fair, very pale, with bright, dark eyes, and light brown hair; very clever and most brilliant in society. I remember my mother saying she was a most lovely girl, but that she lost all her beautiful colour in an illness she had after her engagement with Keats was broken off, 'that mad boy Keats' as they spoke of him then.

It is astonishing to us now to read of the scandalous falsehoods that were then put forward about Keats.

Joseph Severn lay in his grave next to Keats, and many of his letters were unpublished; Fanny Brawne lay in Brompton Cemetery, and her letters to the poet and to the Dilkes had been burnt by Dilke's grandson, Sir Charles Wentworth Dilke, in his parlour fireplace.

William Graham, in the *New Review*, wrote about an interview with Joseph Severn. At this interview – an obvious fake – the aged painter is supposed to have said, "There was certainly no possibility of further life in this world. I did not know it then, but I know it now: that man died of love, if ever a man died of love."

The article continued:

> 'Did Keats ever allude to this cankerworm in anyway to you?' I asked. "Not a word"; the old man gazed out of the window into the depths of the blue Italian sky.

In his supposed interview, Graham also wrote that Severn had dismissed Fanny Brawne as 'flighty and flirting'.

When the fictitious conversation appeared in the *Literary World*, Mrs Perrins reached for her pen:

> Dear Editor,
> Poor Fanny Brawne! 'Flighty and flirting' what a dreadful thing it is to be beloved by a genius! It seems as if people thought they could add to his merits by detracting from hers. I do not believe she was flighty, or she would not have become the clever, brilliant woman I remember; as to flirting I can't say, but Thackeray says, in the heading to one of his stories:
>
>> That other girls besides princesses
>> Like to flirt, the author guesses.
>
> But as Mr Severn knew her so well, did he flirt with her? I am sure she was very much attached to Keats, as she had an illness when the engagement was broken off, which nearly cost her life. Most people said; my mother amongst the rest, who was her great friend, that Mrs Brawne was quite right to wish to put an end to it, as Keats was not able to keep a wife. 'Even geniuses can't live on love and poetry and his health was so bad he was not likely to return from Rome.

A few weeks later the vigilant old lady reappeared in the *Hampstead and Highgate Express*, where she issued a reassuring bulletin. She said she would be sorry for lovers of Keats to think that the lady of his choice was anything but a refined and cultured gentlewoman. In every way, she wrote, Frances Brawne was well fitted to mate with him.

Keats wrote this version of the sonnet 'Bright Star' on a blank page of his Folio Shakespeare, opposite 'A Lover's Complaint'.

Bright Star

Bright star! would I were steadfast as thou art!
Not in lone splendour hung amid the night;
Nor watching, with eternal lids apart
Like Nature's devout sleepless eremite,
The morning waters at their priestlike task
Of pure ablution round earth's human shores;
Or gazing on the new soft fallen mask
Of snow upon the mountains and the moors: –
No – yet still steadfast, still unchangeable,
Cheek-pillow'd on my love's white ripening breast,
To touch, for ever, its warm sink and swell,
Awake, for ever, in a sweet unrest;
To hear, to feel her tender-taken breath,
Half-passionless, and so swoon on to death.

April 1819.

FOOTNOTE: *First version – from John Middleton Murry's limited edition 1929 Poems and Verses of John Keats.*

British Artists, Poets and Writers: Contemporaries of John Keats

AUSTEN, JANE (1775–1817) Author. Born in the rectory at Steventon, Hampshire. Of her novels, *Pride and Prejudice* (1797) is perhaps the best and most widely read. Others include *Sense and Sensibility, Northanger Abbey, Mansfield Park* and *Emma*. In all her books the author reveals a sly sense of humour. Exciting incidents are rare, but her characters are intensely alive.

BARRETT, ELIZABETH (1806–61) Author. Born at Coxhoe-Hall near Durham. As a child she wrote plays in French and English. Aged just fourteen she composed an epic on the Battle of Marathon. Elizabeth was a linguist, mastering several languages. As a young woman she had a fall from her horse and for a long time she was an invalid, confined to the house at 50 Wimpole Street, London, where she was in the care of her repressive father. This stage of her life was depicted in the play *The Barretts of Wimpole Street*. In 1846 she eloped with Robert Browning, the poet, taking with her Wilson (her personal maid) and Flush (her pet dog). The couple lived in Florence, Italy. Elizabeth's poetry is full of fervour. *Sonnets from the Portuguese*, 'Aurora Leigh', 'The Cry of the Children' and 'Cowpers Grave' are well known.

BYRON, GEORGE NOEL GORDON (Lord) (1788–1824). Romantic poet. Born in London. The Byrons were an unstable family. Byron's father spent his wife's fortune and then deserted her. Byron was raised by his mother, his father having died in 1791 when the boy was just three years old. His mother, a Scot from Aberdeenshire, was selfish and argumentative and Byron was ashamed of her, blaming her for his lameness, which he felt set him apart form his fellows. In his early years he lived in poverty in Aberdeen, but at the age of ten he came into property at Newstead Abbey in Nottinghamshire. At Harrow he read classical literature and was a recognised mischief-maker. Later, at Cambridge University, he kept a bear, which he said would become a fellow of the college. He was apt to gamble, and, despite his deformed foot, played cricket well and was a good swimmer. In 1809, with his friend Hobson, Byron went abroad for two years. In 1815 he married. The union was not a happy one and in 1816 his wife left him. After this he moved abroad and never returned. His works of note are *Hours of Idleness* (1807) and *Childe Harold's Pilgrimage* (1812), an account of his travels, which created a sensation. Later works, such as *Don Juan* and *The Vision of Judgement*, scandalised the nation. In England his poetry has never been regarded as of the highest quality; however, on the Continent it has received enthusiastic acclaim. Byron was noted for his 'aristocratic rebelliousness' and an apparent hatred of all mankind. He had a deep conviction of his own irremediable wickedness. These characteristics show in his poetry, as well as a Continental type of romanticism, which ran against the trend in English and Scottish literature at the time. In 1823 he went to Greece to take part in the Greek War of Independence against Turkey. He died of fever at Missolonghi on 19 April 1824.

CARLYLE, THOMAS (1795–1881) Author and historian. Born at Ecclefechan, Dumfriesshire. He studied German literature, he wrote essays and is known for his *Sartor Resartus* (Latin for 'the tailor reclothed'). In 1835 he completed a huge work on the French Revolution. At one point he left the manuscript in the care of his friend J. S. Mill, whose illiterate servant unfortunately used it for lighting fires! Carlyle spent the next year in rewriting it. After 1834 he lived in Cheyne Row, Chelsea, winning fame as a lecturer. His later works included *On Heroes, Hero-Worship and the Heroic in History*; *Oliver Cromwell's Letters and Speeches*; *Past and Present*; and his *History of Frederick II of Prussia*. Carlyle spoke in broad plain Scots, and had difficulty in expressing himself, except in the written word. He admired the strength and virility of figures such as Byron and Napoleon – hence the criticism that he was a forerunner of Nazism in his political thought.

CLARE, JOHN (1793–1864) Poet. Born at Helpston, near Peterborough, Northamptonshire. A casual labourer, he spent most of his life in the countryside. He suffered a series of severe nervous breakdowns and spent the last twenty years of his life in an asylum at Northampton. He had the same publisher as John Keats: Taylor and Hessey, who published his first volume of *Poems Descriptive of Rural Life and Scenery* (1820). This volume was highly successful. It was followed by *The Village Minstrel* (1821), *The Shepherd's Calendar* (1827) and *The Rural Muse* (1835). His last work was published, posthumously, in 1935. Although Clare was a successful poet, he did not receive the benefits of his work, and was always poor.

COBBETT, WILLIAM (1763–1835) Writer and politician. Born at Farnham, Surrey. He won fame with his *History of the Protestant Reformation* (1824–7) and his *Rural Rides* (1830). From 1804 he was a fearless critic of the government, and he was repeatedly imprisoned for libel. He edited his own weekly: the *Weekly Political Register*. He was a recognised champion of farm labourers.

COLERIDGE, SAMUEL TAYLOR (1772–1834) Poet. Born at Ottery St Mary, Devon. After his father died, Samuel, an idle and self-centred child was brought up by an overindulgent uncle. As a young boy he attended Christ's Hospital School and then Cambridge. His life was marked by his emotional instability. He was prone to be fickle and was unable to sustain intellectual effort.

He was recognised as a gifted and excellent talker, and his friends thought highly of him. He married in 1795, but the marriage was not a happy one. In 1797 he met and became a friend of Wordsworth – a friendship that lasted until death parted them. They jointly published *Lyrical Ballads* (1798), to which Coleridge contributed 'The Rime of the Ancient Mariner' and other poems. Soon afterwards his health deteriorated and he began using opium to alleviate the pain that he was suffering. He partially succeeded in breaking the habit, but his mental and physical condition overwhelmed him and he relapsed. The opium reduced his mental power, and this shows in his later work. His best known poems are 'The Rime of the Ancient Mariner' and 'Christabel'. 'Kubla Khan' was composed whilst he was in an opium-induced dream. For the most part, Coleridge's poetry is dream-like and has little connection with the real world. Up until 1819 he gave lectures that were open to the public – lectures on philosophy, literature and Shakespeare. After his son was disgraced and sent down from Oxford – an episode that he took particularly badly – Coleridge gave up writing, but people still flocked to his talks. According to Carlyle, Coleridge's talk was mostly 'the mistiest, wide, unintelligible deluge of things'. However, there is no doubt that he made a huge impression on his contemporaries. Charles Lamb described him as 'an Archangel, a little damaged'.

CONSTABLE, JOHN (1776–1837) Artist. Born at East Bergholt, Suffolk. He is particularly noted as a painter of Suffolk scenes. His most famous pictures include *The Hay Wain* (1821), *Salisbury Cathedral*, *The Leaping Horse* and *Dedham Vale*. He was a master at depicting the charm of rural England and the changing panorama of the wide East Anglian sky. Although he was much appreciated in France during his lifetime, he died before his own people recognised him as one of their greatest landscape painters.

CRABBE, GEORGE (1754–1832) Poet. Born at Aldeburgh, Suffolk. Aldeburgh at the time was a half-ruined fishing village. His family was very poor. His father was a collector of salt duties. George was the eldest of six children. His father, who had a knowledge of mathematics, was also something of a philosopher and subscribed to *Martin's Philosophical Magazine*, which had a 'poets' corner'; Crabbe wrote his first verses in imitation of what he found there. After several menial jobs, in 1771, aged just seventeen, he was apprenticed to a surgeon at Woodbridge. After leaving Woodbridge, he travelled to London, where he lived very poorly. He haunted the hospitals, endeavouring to improve his medical knowledge without paying for it. Crabbe lived as a self-taught apothecary, a clergyman and a poet. He struggled to find publishers and patrons for his writing. In 1780 he published a poem entitled *The Candidate*, and a year later he was in danger of imprisonment for debt. In 1783 his poem *The Village* was published, which he wrote with his own village (Aldeburgh) in mind. This was followed by *The Newspaper* (1785). For the most part, Crabbe wrote long poems based on places and happenings in his life. They did not sell well and the Crabbe family were always poor. In 1813, Mira, his wife, died. In 1819 John Murray, the publisher, offered him £3,000 for the copyright of his poems and to publish his last book, *Tales of the Hall*. Crabbe died in 1832 at the age of seventy-eight.

CROME, JOHN (1768–1821) Artist. Born at Norwich, Norfolk. He excelled at landscape paintings.

DIBDIN, CHARLES (1745–1814) Songwriter and entertainer. born at Southampton. He wrote over 600 songs, including 'Tom Bowling' and 'Poor Jack'.

DICKENS, CHARLES (1812–70) Novelist, playwright and public reader. Born at Portsea near Portsmouth. He moved to Chatham in 1816. Later, in London, the family became so poor that they often pawned their clothes, and as a child Charles was sent to work in a blacking factory, where he earned six shillings a week. When his family were sent to a debtors' prison, Charles was cared for by an old lady in Camden Town. After a brief schooling, Dickens became a clerk in a solicitor's office, where he studied shorthand. In 1832 he reported on parliamentary speeches, and about the same time began writing sketches on London life for the *Evening Chronicle* under the pen-name of Boz. In 1836 he became famous as the author of the serialised story *The Pickwick Papers*. This was the first of many books that in the beginning appeared in serial form. He married Catherine Hogarth, but the marriage was not a happy one and they separated after twenty years. However, the union produced ten children, and Dickens found fatherhood a great comfort to him. He went to America in 1842 and was fêted wherever he went. At the height of his fame he bought a house, Gad's Hill, in Kent. By 1865 he was suffering from a nervous condition brought on by a railway accident. However, he continued to give popular readings from his books. His well-known novels include *The Pickwick Papers*, *Oliver Twist*, *Nicholas Nickleby*, *The Old Curiosity Shop*, *Barnaby Rudge*, *Martin Chuzzlewit*, *A Christmas Carol*, *David Copperfield*, *Bleak House*, *Little Dorrit*, *A Tale of Two Cities*, *Great Expectations* and the unfinished *Mystery of Edwin Drood*. Dickens died at Gad's Hill in 1870.

FITZGERALD, EDWARD (1809–83) Poet. Born near Woodbridge, Suffolk. His greatest work is a poem translation of the Persian *Rubaiyat of Omar Khayyám* (1859). He was a friend of Thackeray, Carlyle, Rossetti, Tennyson and Swinburne.

HAZLITT, WILLIAM (1778–1830) Essayist and critic. Born at Maidstone, Kent. He was a friend of Coleridge, Wordsworth and Charles Lamb. In 1812 he became a parliamentary reporter. In 1817 he published *A View of the English Stage* and *Lectures on the English Poets*. His other books include *Characters of Shakespeare's Plays*. In 1821-2 he edited the magazine *Table*

Talk. He established a reputation as a critic, essayist and lecturer. His best work is regarded as the later collection of essays *The Spirit of the Age* (1825). In spite of his moody, difficult character, he was held in high regard by those who counted themselves his friends.

HUNT, LEIGH (1784–1859) Poet and writer. Born near London. Editor, with his brother John, of *The Examiner*. Both men were imprisoned for libel against the Prince Regent. He was a friend of Keats, Shelley, Charles Lamb, Hazlitt and other literary figures.

KEAN, EDMUND (c.1787–1833) Actor. Born in London. He was noted for his mastery of tragic Shakespearean characters, such as Shylock and Richard III. Coleridge said that his acting was 'like reading Shakespeare by flashes of lightning'. He was greatly admired by Keats.

LAMB, CHARLES (1775–1834) and **MARY** (1764–1847) Brother and sister famous in English literature. Charles was born at the Crown Office Row, Inner Temple, London. He was educated at Christ's Hospital school, where during his schooldays he was friendly with Coleridge. He was employed for thirty-three years as a clerk in East India House, and made every effort to support his somewhat poor family. Mary, a writer of merit in her own right, suffered from a nervous condition. Under the strain of working for little money to supplement the family's income, and at the same time running the home because her mother was incapable of doing so, she suffered a severe nervous breakdown. While mentally unbalanced, she stabbed her mother through the heart. She was lucky to escape imprisonment, being committed to an asylum at Hackney. Charles loved her dearly, and he pleaded for her release into his care, which was granted. Charles added to their finances by contributing to various publications, and Mary wrote the acclaimed *Tales from Shakespeare*. From 1820, Charles wrote essays for the *London Magazine* – the *Essays of Elia* (1823–

33) – which were later published in book form and became the most admired and recognised of his work. Charles is also remembered as a poet, letter-writer and wit. Examples of his witticisms include 'half as sober as a judge', 'The greatest pleasure I know, is to do a good action by stealth, and to have it found out by accident' also ' "Presents", I often say, "Endear Absents".' He retired from the East India Company in 1825 on a pension of £450 a year, but even in retirement the health of his sister, to whom he had devoted his life, caused him a good deal of anxiety. After a long period of poor health, he died at Edmonton. His sister lived on alone at the edge of reason for a further thirteen years.

LANDOR, WALTER SAVAGE (1775–1864) Poet and writer. Born at Warwick. Landor was the author of various books, including the celebrated *Imaginary Conversations* (1824–9). He was a friend of Byron, Shelley and Charles Armitage Brown. It was Brown who introduced him to literature and assisted him in his writing. Landor severely burnt his hand in plucking Shelley's heart from his funeral pyre. He accompanied Byron on his ill-fated venture to Greece.

LEAR, EDWARD (1812–88) Poet, writer and artist. Born in London. He is most famous for his humorous books and rhymes. *A Book of Nonsense* (1846), with its quaint illustrations, was followed by *More Nonsense Rhymes* (1871). The limerick, a humorous verse of five lines, was made popular by Lear.

MILNES, RICHARD MONCKTON (Lord Houghton) (1809–85) Poet and biographer. Born in London. He was a friend and helper of literary men. He produced the first biography of John Keats (1848).

PAINE, THOMAS (1737–1809) Writer and reformer. Born at Thetford, Norfolk. In his book *The Rights of Man* (1791) he supported the French Revolution. He also made an attack on religion when he wrote *The Age of Reason* (1794).

PROCTER, BRYAN WALLER (1787–1874) Poet, songwriter and biographer. Born at Leeds. He wrote memoirs of Charles Lamb and Edmund Kean under the pen-name of Barry Cornwall. His first book *Dramatic Scenes and Other Poems* was reviewed by Leigh Hunt in *The Examiner*. He sent a copy of this work, together with his second book, *A Sicilian Story*, to Keats. He had a meeting with Keats in 1820 whilst the poet was unwell and staying at Leigh Hunt's house. Hunt said that Procter was very impressed with the poet's personality. Outside of the close literary circle, Procter is recognised for his songwriting.

SCOTT, SIR WALTER (1771–1832) Novelist and poet. Born in Edinburgh. He wrote romantic poems of the old days in Scotland, such as *The Lay of the Last Minstrel* (1805), *The Lady of the Lake* (1810), *Marmion* and *Rokeby*. He became a baronet in 1820, but at the age of fifty-five he suffered a severe setback when James Ballantyne went bankrupt. Scott was a partner in the firm, so he shared the misfortune. A sum of £250,000 was owing – a huge sum at the time. Scott worked to repay every penny, but he ruined his health in the process. After his wife died, he went to Rome for the sake of his health, but returned to Abbotsford, where he died. His son John wrote the life story of his father – Scotland's greatest historical novelist. Sir Walter Scott is buried at Dryburgh Abbey.

SHELLEY, PERCY BYSSHE (1792–1822) Poet. Born near Warnham, Sussex. A rebel at Oxford, he was eager to put the world right! His university career ended because of a pamphlet he produced on atheism (1811). Thrown out of Oxford, he lived in poverty-stricken lodgings in London, where he met and fell in love with Harriet Westbrook, then only sixteen. Shelley eloped with her to Scotland, where they were married. Harriet bore him two children, but the marriage was not happy, and Shelley left her for Mary Wollstonecraft Godwin. Harriet committed suicide, and the scandal damaged Shelley's reputation in the country. The court deemed him an unfit parent and his children were removed from him. From then on he became unwell and moved abroad. Finally, he reached Italy, where he joined Byron. He studied Greek and enjoyed the classics with his loyal friend Thomas Love Peacock. Shelley drowned whilst sailing with a friend, Captain Williams. Their yacht was overwhelmed in a storm while sailing from Leghorn to Spezia. His body was cremated on the beach in the presence of Lord Byron, Leigh Hunt and Walter Landor. Shelley's poetry, like his life, is full of idealism and passion. His *The Revolt of Islam*, *Prometheus Unbound* and *The Cenci* (a tragedy) are all great poems, but he is chiefly remembered for the poem *Adonais*, written on the death of Keats. Other outstanding works were 'The Cloud' and 'To a Skylark'. Shelley's remains and ashes share the same cemetery in Rome as John Keats.

SHELLEY, MARY (1797–1851) Authoress. She is remembered as the writer of the gruesome story *Frankenstein*.

SIDDONS, SARAH (1755–1831) Actress. Born at Brecon, South Wales. She made her first stage appearance at Drury Lane in 1775 playing Portia, and she became the greatest tragic actress of her day.

SMITH, SIDNEY (1771–1845) Author, churchman and Whig politician. Born at Woodford, Essex. A renowned wit, he was the co-founder and editor of The *Edinburgh Review*. In 1831 he was appointed canon of St Paul's.

SOUTHEY, ROBERT (1774–1843) Poet and author. Born at Bristol. In his early life Southey was a rebel and wrote attacking religion and politics. He was very much influenced by the French Revolution and travelled widely in Spain and Portugal. He was a friend of Wordsworth and Coleridge. He became poet laureate in 1813, and is remembered for his book *The Life of Nelson*. Southey died insane.

TENNYSON, ALFRED (Lord) (1809–92) Poet. Born at The Rectory, Somersby, Lincolnshire. He was educated at Louth Grammar School and Cambridge University. Whilst at Cambridge, he became a friend and admirer of Arthur Henry Hallam (1811–33), who was a genius, knew several languages and wrote plays and poems. Hallam died suddenly in Vienna while still a young man. Tennyson was greatly shocked, and later, in 1850, the year he became poet laureate, he published a long poem 'In Memoriam' as a tribute to his great friend. Tennyson's notable works include 'The Princess', 'Maud' and the *Idylls of the King*, a series of poems about King Arthur and the Knights of the Round Table. His shorter poems include 'The Lady of Shalott' (1833), 'The Lotos-Eaters' (1833), 'Break, Break, Break' (1842) and 'The Charge of the Light Brigade' (1854). His last poem, 'Crossing the Bar' (1889), was sung at his funeral in Westminster Abbey.

TURNER, JOSEPH MALLORD WILLIAM (1775–1851) Artist. Born in London. Regarded by some as the world's greatest landscape painter, Turner was the son of a barber. He made excellent drawings when only a young boy, and at the age of fifteen he exhibited at the Royal Academy. He walked all over England, studying the skies and scenery, and he travelled thoughout Germany and Italy. In Italy he saw the old masters, and the special light of that sunny land inspired him. Turner, apart from his painting, also advanced the art of engraving. He was elected to the Royal Academy in 1802. Although a genius and very rich, he was a lonely man and never married. He had had a poor education, which made him painfully shy and reserved. When asked about his art, he is said to have replied, "Well, painting's a rum thing." Turner excelled in both watercolour and oil paint. He painted literally hundreds of pictures of English and foreign scenes, and he is especially noted for his seascapes. He died at Chelsea and donated his pictures to the nation.

WORDSWORTH, WILLIAM (1770–1850) Poet. Born at Cockermouth, Cumberland. Wordsworth was orphaned at fourteen. He had, even then, a deep love of nature and would wander alone in the Lake District, enjoying the open countryside. In 1798 he joined his friend Coleridge in publishing *Lyrical Ballads*, in which the two poets aimed to free poetry from the stilted language in vogue at the time. Wordsworth wrote poetry about ordinary things and events that the simplest folk could understand. When the French Revolution began he was in France, and his thirteen months of study came to an abrupt end. The event affected him deeply, and from then on he looked for freedom for all men. Wordsworth did a great service to English literature, reviving a love of nature and bringing natural simplicity to poetry. However, at times he was over-simple and too wordy, saying with poetry what would have been better in prose. He rose to great heights in his sonnets; for example, 'Upon Westminster Bridge' and 'Valedictory Sonnet to the River Duddon' (1820). His greatest poems include *The Prelude*, *The Excursion*, 'Tintern Abbey' and the 'Ode on the Intimations of Immortality'. Wordsworth married Mary Hutchinson in 1802, and they lived for a time at Dove Cottage, Grasmere, Westmoreland. Keats called at Dove Cottage in July 1818, only to find that the poet and his family were out. Wordsworth was happy in his marriage, fortunate in the complete devotion and love of his wife. He wrote about their first meeting, describing his first impression of her as 'a phantom of delight'. His sister Dorothy (1771–1855), who Keats said was beautiful, lived with and supported him her entire life. She was educated and literate, and she is recognised for her journals. Wordsworth was appointed poet laureate in 1843.

Keats Poems Mentioned in This Book

On the Sea
You Say You Love
Hush, Hush! Tread Softly!
Hyperion
Bright Star
The Eve of St Agnes
The Eve of St Mark
The Cap and Bells
Lines to Fanny
Ode to Fanny
The Day Is Gone
This Living Hand
Isabella (*or* The Pot of Basil)
Otho the Great
Lamia
Written on the Day That Mr Leigh Hunt Left Prison
Imitation of Spenser
On First Looking into Chapman's Homer
Sleep and Poetry
Endymion
Ode to Psyche
Ode on Melancholy
Ode on Indolence
Ode to a Nightingale
Ode on a Grecian Urn
On Fame
To Autumn